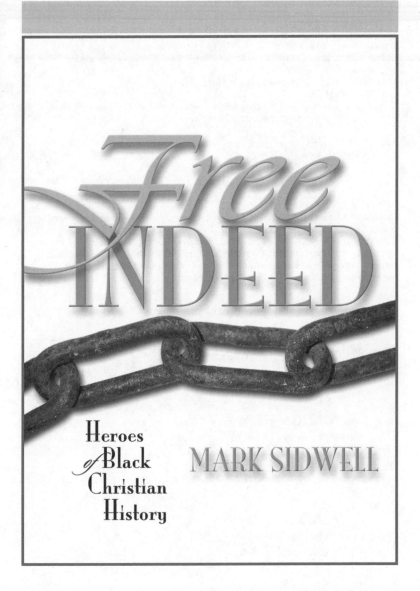

Free INDEED

Heroes of Black Christian History

MARK SIDWELL

D0905569

BJU PRESS

Greenville, South Carolina

Library of Congress Cataloging-in-Publication Data

Sidwell, Mark, 1958-
    Free indeed : heroes of Black Christian history / Mark Sidwell.—Expanded ed.
    p. cm.
    Includes bibliographical references and index.
    ISBN 1-57924-734-2
    1. African American clergy—Biography—Juvenile literature. 2. Clergy—United
States—Biography—Juvenile literature. I. Title.

BR563.N4 S53 2001
277.3'0089'96073—dc21
[B]

                                                                    2001049939

NOTE:
The fact that materials produced by other publishers are referred to in this volume does not constitute an endorsement by Bob Jones University Press of the content or theological position of materials produced by such publishers. The position of Bob Jones University Press, and the University itself, is well known. Any references and ancillary materials are listed as an aid to the reader and in an attempt to maintain the accepted academic standards of the publishing industry.

All Scripture is quoted from the Authorized King James Version.

Free Indeed: Heroes of Black Christian History
Mark Sidwell, Ph.D.

Edited by Christa Habegger
Composition by Peggy Hargis
Cover design by Chris Hartzler
Illustrations by Ruth Pearson Ventrello
Photographs by Unusual Films (church), Chris Hartzler (chain)

© 2001 Bob Jones University Press
Greenville, South Carolina 29614

ISBN 1-57924-734-2

15   14   13   12   11   10   9   8   7   6   5   4   3   2   1

Contents

INTRODUCTION

"Let us now praise famous men," wrote Jesus ben Sirach two centuries before Christ was born, speaking of the heroes of Jewish history. "All these were honored in their generations, and were the glory of their times." He said, "Their seed shall remain for ever, and their glory shall not be blotted out. Their bodies are buried in peace; but their name liveth for evermore."

Free Indeed: Heroes of Black Christian History is an effort to give due notice to African Americans who were faithful followers of Jesus Christ, who were the glory of *their* times. They are men whose lives, to use the words of Jonathan Edwards, are a means of "representing and recommending true religion and virtue to the world . . . by . . . instance and example."

The title of this work derives from the words of Jesus: "Verily, verily, I say unto you, Whosoever committeth sin is the servant of sin. And the servant abideth not in the house for ever: but the Son abideth ever. If the Son therefore shall make you free, ye shall be free indeed" (John 8:34-36). Ironically, Christians are free and "enslaved" at the same time. Jesus Christ declares that those He frees from sin are truly free. Yet all Christians are "servants" (literally slaves) of Christ. Paul said, "For he that is called in the Lord, being a servant, is the Lord's freeman: likewise also he that is called, being free, is Christ's servant" (I Cor. 7:22; see also Rom. 1:1; 6:16-22; II Tim. 2:24). A member of the congregation of John Jasper, black minister in Richmond, Virginia, after the Civil War, said of her pastor, "He always thought of hisself as the servant of King Jesus. That was a slavery that he liked and never wished to get free from it."

But to be a voluntary slave of Christ is much different from being forcibly enslaved by another man or suffering oppression solely because of one's race. With the exception of C. P. Jones and the native African Samuel Morris, all the subjects of this book lived when slavery was legal in America. Some were actually slaves for a time, and all suffered some form of discrimination because of their race. Nearly every one of them therefore worked in some way to uplift the members of his race to positions of dignity as human beings and equality as American citizens.

There have been many men of all races who have striven to uplift the downtrodden of this world. But the men presented in this book are also notable as heroes of *Christian* history. They display the work of God's grace in their lives and testify of that grace to others. Being freed from sin, they were *free indeed*. Daniel Payne, a bishop of the

AME Church, said to those liberated by the abolition of slavery in the District of Columbia, "As you are now free in body, so now seek to be free in soul and spirit, from sin and Satan. The *noblest freeman is he whom Christ makes free.*"

The Black Church in America

The history of the black church in America is a story of faith in God and the triumph of His power. Although African Americans have a distinct heritage and have made important contributions to American history, many historians have seen the church as the most important black institution in American life not only as a religious force but also as a social and political force. The civil rights movement, for example, has found some of its greatest strength and support in the churches. Furthermore, Christians ought to study every display of God's grace. African Americans should be aware of their rich Christian heritage, and Christians of other races should not allow barriers of race or class to keep them from appreciating the work of God among those who differ from them.

RISE OF THE BLACK CHURCH (1619-1865)

The arrival of a load of twenty slaves in Jamestown, Virginia, in 1619 marked the beginning of America's shameful involvement with slavery, and it is mostly as slaves that Africans were introduced to America. Against this backdrop of oppression and suffering, the black church in America had its beginnings. Some blacks received their freedom through the kindness of compassionate masters who set them free. Others were freed as the Northern states abolished slavery. Some escaped slavery and found liberty in the free areas of the North or in Canada. But the majority of African Americans remained slaves, and even those who were free usually faced discrimination, existing only as second-class citizens in the eyes of most of the white majority.

There is little record of black religious life for the first century and a half of American history. Apparently, most blacks (including the small number of free blacks) attended the white churches when they attended at all, usually sitting in racially segregated sections of the white churches, such as the balcony. This situation began to change with the Great Awakening, the great revival that swept the British colonies of North America in the middle part of the eighteenth century. Powerful preachers of the gospel such as Massachusetts pastor Jonathan Edwards and British evangelist George Whitefield led many to Christ. Among those converted were many

1

blacks, especially as a result of Whitefield's ministry. It is from the period during and just after the Great Awakening that we have our first records of widespread conversion of blacks to Christianity and of the formation of black churches.

Black Churches in the South

The first independent black churches were formed in the South among the Baptists. There is some controversy about when the first black church was founded. The earliest was apparently begun around 1774 by former slaves George Liele (c. 1750-1828) and David George (1742-1810) in Silver Bluff, South Carolina. After Liele went to Jamaica as a missionary and George went to Canada, one of their converts, Andrew Bryan (1737-1812), began the first lasting black work in the South—the First African Baptist Church in Savannah, started in 1788.

Blacks in the South often faced white opposition to their meetings. Andrew Bryan, for example, was once publicly whipped for preaching the gospel in Savannah. But opposition was not widespread at first, and many whites defended the black churches until fear of slave revolts spread across the South. In 1822 in Charleston, South Carolina, former slave Denmark Vesey plotted a slave rebellion. Informers alerted the authorities before it took place, and Vesey and thirty-four others were arrested, tried, and executed. Vesey's leadership in a black Methodist church in Charleston (although the pastor and other leaders apparently knew nothing about the revolt) caused a white mob to burn the church. Even more dramatic was an actual slave rebellion led by a black slave preacher, Nat Turner, in Virginia in 1831. In that insurrection over a hundred and fifty people (black and white) died. Turner's revolt launched a wave of repressive laws limiting and even eliminating the independence of black churches in the South.

Despite the Turner uprising, many Southerners did not want to put an absolute end to black religion. They preferred, however, that blacks hear either white ministers or black preachers who were approved by the slave owners. From 1830 to the beginning of the Civil War, several religious organizations promoted a "religious instruction movement" among blacks, setting up Sunday schools especially for slaves and free blacks. At its worst, this movement simply used religious instruction to try to make slaves submissive by stressing over and over again, "Servants, obey in all things your masters" (Col. 3:22). A former slave ridiculed the sermons she heard from an approved white minister: "The preacher came and . . . he'd just say, 'Serve your masters. Don't steal your master's

2

turkey. Don't steal your master's chickens. Don't steal your master's hawgs. Don't steal your master's meat. Do whatsomever your master tells you to do.' Same old thing all the time."

Some white Christians, however, took seriously their responsibility to preach the gospel to everyone. The most famous of these ministers to the slaves was Charles Colcock Jones (1804-63), sometimes called "Apostle to the Slaves." He conducted an extensive ministry among the plantations in Georgia, preaching the gospel and establishing "missions" among the slaves. Jones did not ignore the idea of slaves being "good servants," but that emphasis was small in comparison to his stress on the whole of Christian doctrine and life. Jones seems to have had serious reservations about slavery and in his private correspondence hinted that preaching the gospel to slaves might hasten the end of slavery. He sought, however, to work within the confines of southern slavery and never directly challenged the institution.

Many slaves, despite the dangers, continued to hold secret services of their own. Historians have called these underground churches the "invisible institution" of slave religion. Silently and secretly, slaves would sneak away to services held in the woods and hollows. There, despite the need for quiet, they could preach, sing, and praise God without any white master to stand by and pass judgment on what they did. After the Civil War, the few independent black churches, the blacks attending white churches, the missions established by men such as Jones, and the "invisible institution" of secret slave worship all blended to provide the basis for flourishing independent black churches in the South.

One of the lasting heritages of black religion in the South was the spiritual, a religious folksong expressing the deep yearnings of the slaves. Many spirituals have been preserved for us: "Go Down, Moses," "Swing Low, Sweet Chariot," "Steal Away to Jesus," and "Were You There?" to name a few. The spirituals expressed an intense emotional devotion to God. Some writers have claimed that spirituals were nothing more than disguised pleas for an end to slavery. This element was certainly present, as shown in "Go Down, Moses":

When Israel was in Egypt's land—
Let My people go!
Oppressed so hard they could not stand—
Let My people go!

Go down, Moses,
Way down in Egypt land,
To tell old Pharaoh, To let My people go!

But the lyrics of these songs also clearly contained worship and praise to God, exhortations to love Christ and be like Him, and earnest prayers for strength. The often mournful melodies derive from folksongs, camp meeting songs, standard hymns, and perhaps even some African tunes. The spiritual represents the African American supplication to God, reflected through the lens of the black American experience.

Black Churches in the North

The situation for blacks in the North before the Civil War was somewhat better. Slavery eventually died out in that section, and antislavery sentiment was often strong there. Northern blacks enjoyed some opportunities that Southern blacks did not have. Prejudice was very real, though, as evidenced in the origin of the leading independent black denominations before the Civil War. Former slave Richard Allen (1760-1831) worked with great success among blacks in Philadelphia. The predominantly white Methodist church to which he belonged, however, grew to resent the increasing number of blacks in its congregation. Allen and his followers walked out of a service after church officials tried to forcibly move a black member to a seat in the back of the balcony during prayer. They formed their own church and eventually their own denomination—the African Methodist Episcopal (AME) Church, the largest black Methodist group.

Another group formed in the North, similar in structure—and name—to Allen's group, was the African Methodist Episcopal Zion (AMEZ) Church. Under the leadership of men such as James Varick (1750?-1828), its first bishop, the group likewise sought to establish churches in which blacks could worship free from scorn and discrimination. The AMEZ Church became home to some of the leading black antislavery advocates, including Frederick Douglass (1817-95), Sojourner Truth (1797?-1883), and Harriet Tubman (1820?-1913).

The Baptists also attracted many African Americans. In this period, however, black Baptists were known not so much for organized denominations as for individual churches. Pioneer church planter Thomas Paul (1773-1831) founded two notable churches: the Joy Street Baptist Church in Boston (1805) and the Abyssinian Baptist Church in New York City (1808). The latter has become

4

one of the most famous and influential black Baptist churches in America.

Almost all northern black churches, even the most doctrinally conservative, promoted social and political efforts to gain freedom and political rights for blacks. They became particularly active in the movement for the abolition of slavery. Black churches in the North supported antislavery groups, and their buildings often served as refuges for escaped slaves. The black churches also provided some of the most eloquent orators of the abolition movement. This antislavery activity set a pattern for later black political activity.

EMANCIPATION, EXPANSION, AND OPPOSITION (1865-1954)

Rights and Repression

The end of the Civil War brought many gains to American blacks. By the Thirteenth, Fourteenth, and Fifteenth Amendments to the Constitution, slavery was abolished and blacks were granted—theoretically—the same rights and privileges of citizenship as whites. During the Reconstruction era (1865-77), African Americans held political office in the South and established schools in the region. Poverty remained a problem for the freed slaves, however, and after 1877 the federal government took less interest in the situation of southern blacks. A series of Supreme Court decisions in the late nineteenth century permitted the creation of segregated ("separate but equal") facilities for blacks in schools, transportation, hotels, and restaurants. Southern states passed laws racially segregating virtually all settings, even restrooms and drinking fountains. States also used literacy tests and poll taxes to discourage blacks from voting. An example of the effects of legislation to limit black voting can be seen in Louisiana. In 1896 there were over 130,000 blacks registered to vote. By 1900 the number had plummeted to slightly more than 1,300.

After 1900, and particularly after World War I, many blacks began to move to northern cities in search of work and greater freedom. Historians sometimes refer to this move as the "Great Migration." Unquestionably this shift drastically altered the black experience in America. It was not simply a matter of shifting northward but of changing from a predominantly rural to a predominantly urban way of life. With this change often came social and economic improvement. But unfortunately African Americans

5

sometimes found northern whites as unsympathetic as many in the South.

The Black Preacher as Leader

This lower place of blacks in American society explains another characteristic of black religion: the leading role of the church and the pastor in black culture. The churches were sometimes the only institutions that blacks could call completely their own. The pastor therefore became a community leader, and many of the most talented blacks aspired to be ministers. Often the best of African American talent was found in the pulpit. For example, the first black in the United States Senate, Hiram Revels (1822-1901) of Mississippi, was a minister in the African Methodist Episcopal Church.

Black preachers tended to divide between conservatives and progressives. Critics say that many conservatives seemed to strive more to please the white majority than to serve the needs of their congregations. African American diplomat Ralph Bunche recalled meeting a black pastor in the South who said, "We are the policemen of the Negroes. If we did not keep down their ambitions and divert them into religion, there would be upheaval in the South." Many conservatives, however, preferred simply to be left alone to minister to their flocks. John Jasper (1812-1901) of Richmond, Virginia, was one such man. Having known the trials of life under slavery, he was content to enjoy the new freedom to preach the gospel without limitations. Progressives sometimes tended to be theologically liberal, but many were orthodox men who nonetheless devoted themselves to improving the status of African Americans. Presbyterians Matthew Anderson (1845-1928) and Francis Grimké (1850-1937) and Methodist Daniel Payne (1811-93) are examples of orthodox progressives. Some black pastors fell between these two groups. These ministers, such as Philadelphia Methodist Charles Tindley (1851-1933), concentrated on the church's ministry to evangelize the lost and to edify the saints, but they also devoted considerable effort to social relief.

Denominational Growth

The era after the Civil War saw the growth of new black denominations and the enlargement of the old ones. Probably the most important event was the union of three separate groups to form the National Baptist Convention, U.S.A., Inc., in 1895. Many events contributed to its origin, but one controversy in particular seemed to justify the need for a separate group. The American

Baptist Publication Society extended an invitation to several black Baptists to write materials for their Sunday school publications. Protests from white Baptists in the South, however, caused the society to withdraw the invitation. The incident led African American Baptists to found their own publication society, an organization that eventually contributed to the formation of the National Baptists. Despite schisms since that time, the National Baptist Convention, U.S.A., has continued to be one of the largest black denominations in the United States.

In the South, blacks had most often worshiped in white churches before the Civil War. Afterwards, black desires for independence and white desires for separation of races led to the creation of new denominations. The most important of these new southern groups was probably the Christian (originally "Colored") Methodist Episcopal (CME) Church. It was formed in 1870 from the black constituency of the Methodist Episcopal Church, South. The CME Church has expanded beyond the South, but it retains its predominantly southern flavor.

The black church also saw growth through the Holiness and Pentecostal movements. The Holiness movement began in the late nineteenth century. Many Methodists thought that their church was losing its zeal for God, especially the zeal for holiness. Holiness Christians taught that after conversion, the Holy Spirit in a special "second work of grace" (after the first work of salvation) cleansed the saint of all traces of the sinful nature inherited from Adam. Sin was "eradicated," and a believer could live free from known sin. The teaching appealed to many African Americans, not only Methodists but also Baptists and other groups. Several black Holiness denominations grew out of this movement, such as the Church of the Living God, formed in 1889, and the Church of Christ (Holiness), U.S.A., formed in 1907.

The Pentecostal movement grew out of the Holiness movement. Like the Holiness movement, Pentecostalism sought further "gifts of the Spirit" after conversion. Because their most distinctive practice was "speaking in tongues," these Christians took the name Pentecostal from the events on the Day of Pentecost, described in Acts 2. Traditionally, the modern Pentecostal movement is said to have begun in 1900 in a Holiness Bible college in Topeka, Kansas, where students began speaking in tongues. The real growth, however, came through the Azusa Street Revival in Los Angeles from 1906 to 1909. Led by black Holiness preacher William Seymour (1870-1922), the services featured displays of tongues speaking that attracted both the merely curious and the deeply interested.

The fame of "the Azusa Street revival" gave momentum to the young movement. Indeed, some historians believe that Seymour deserves the real credit for founding Pentecostalism.

Pentecostalism proved enormously popular among blacks. Small congregations began springing up across the country, particularly in northern cities with large black populations. Unable to afford fine buildings, Pentecostal churches rented unused stores in poorer commercial districts. When blacks moved north into the large cities, they often found that they felt more comfortable in the informal, humble storefront Pentecostal churches than in the churches of the more established denominations.

The most important black Pentecostal group has been the Church of God in Christ. Founded by Bishop Charles Harrison Mason (1866-1961) in 1907, the denomination blends Pentecostal teaching, traditional black worship practices, and strict standards of Christian behavior. Despite criticism of these standards, the church has grown rapidly. It grew nearly fifty percent between 1982 and 1991 and is now not only one of the largest black denominations in America but also one of the largest denominations of any kind in the United States.

Black Intellectualism and the Church

At the beginning of the twentieth century, there were new intellectual currents among African Americans that were not always sympathetic to the church. A major black leader was W. E. B. Du Bois (1868-1963). A leader in the Niagara Movement and a founder of the NAACP (National Association for the Advancement of Colored People), Du Bois called for greater political action and the pursuit of higher education by American blacks. Du Bois often criticized what he saw as the social conservatism of the black church. The churches, he thought, were too content to stress a "heavenly by and by" and not deal with the present problems of African Americans. Du Bois also influenced an important black cultural movement, the Harlem Renaissance. The writers and poets of this movement achieved notice beyond the bounds of the black community through their writings rooted in the American black experience. They also often shared Du Bois's disdain for the alleged conservatism of the black church.

This opposition to the role of the church, however, did not always result in total disregard for what the church meant to the black community. The authors of the Harlem Renaissance often appreciated the church as an essential part of the African American heritage. A good illustration is *God's Trombones,* a series of poems by James Weldon Johnson (1871-1938) based on the sermons he heard as a child. The poems capture well the substance and style of black sermons. Johnson said in his preface, "The old-time Negro preacher has not yet been given the niche in which he properly belongs. . . . It was through him that the people of diverse languages and customs who were brought here from diverse parts of Africa and thrown into slavery were given their first sense of unity and solidarity. He was the first shepherd of the bewildered flock. His power for good or ill was very great. It was the old-time preacher who for generations was the mainspring of hope and inspiration for the Negro in America." Johnson's poems—including "Listen, Lord—A Prayer," "The Creation," "Go Down Death—A Funeral Sermon," and "The Judgment Day"—treat their scriptural topics with respect and provide a sense of the power and sincerity of black preaching.

Rise of Gospel Music

One cultural development in the urban black church of the North was the growth of "black gospel" music. People use the phrase "gospel music" in many senses. In the nineteenth century, for example, the "gospel songs" of composers such as Fanny Crosby and Ira Sankey took their place in the churches alongside the more formal hymns of composers such as Charles Wesley and Isaac Watts. From the American South came "southern gospel," a blend of bluegrass, folk, and country and western music that emerged about the same time as black gospel.

In some circles, however, the term "gospel music" is virtually equivalent to "black gospel." The father of black gospel music was Thomas Dorsey (1899-1993). A musician, Dorsey was torn between his love for blues and jazz, musical styles that had developed among urban blacks, and church music. He tried writing music for both the church and the nightclub. Finally, after a conversion experience in 1928, he devoted himself to writing music for God. Yet, even then, he blended elements of blues and jazz to create a distinct sound. One can almost date the birth of black gospel with the writing of Dorsey's "Precious Lord, Take My Hand" (1932), penned in deep distress after he lost his wife and newborn son. He went on to write other songs, such as "Peace in the Valley," that helped established the black gospel sound. Black gospel became the music of the African American church in the twentieth century just as the spiritual had been the music of the black church in the nineteenth.

Cults and "Alternate Religions"

Not all religious growth among blacks has been Christian. Cults have made major inroads in the African American community. Often predominantly "white" cults such as Jehovah's Witnesses won black members because blacks sensed that they were treated more readily as equals than in many white churches. Other cults are distinctively black. Major Jealous Divine (often called "Father Divine"; 1865?-1965) was one of the most famous cult leaders. With his headquarters on Long Island, Divine was believed to be God incarnate by followers. Since his death, his followers have continued to believe he will return.

Probably even better known to the public is the Nation of Islam, commonly called the "Black Muslims." A mixture of Islamic teaching and black nationalism, the group was founded by Master Wali Fard Muhammad (Wallace Fard) in 1930 but really built by Elijah Poole, who took the name "Elijah Muhammad" (1897-1975). Muhammad, who led the group from 1934 to his death, taught that whites were a "devil race" accidentally created by a "mad black scientist." The group's most famous member, Malcolm X (1925-65), eventually left to form his own sect. He was later assassinated, and the Black Muslims were implicated in the crime. After Elijah Muhammad's death, later leaders changed the name to American Muslim Mission and tried to conform more to orthodox Islamic teaching. However, a minority faction kept the name Nation of Islam and followed Louis Farrakhan, who maintained the black exclusivism of the original group.

CIVIL RIGHTS, BLACK PRIDE, AND THE CHURCH (SINCE 1954)

Civil Rights Movement

The growth of the Black Muslims reflects the increased emphasis on black consciousness of pride in their heritage. This mood has grown since the 1950s with the dramatic emergence of the civil rights movement. Technically, a civil right is a specific privilege or entitlement that is granted by law. The government is responsible for protecting these rights from both government and individual encroachment. In modern American history, the phrase "civil rights movement" refers primarily to attempts by blacks to secure the exercise and protection of their civil rights.

In 1954 the Supreme Court ordered an end to segregated schools in the case *Brown* v. *Board of Education.* This event marked the beginning of the modern civil rights movement. Other court decisions quickly followed banning other forms of racial discrimination. Then in 1955 blacks in Montgomery, Alabama, protested segregated seating in public buses by boycotting Montgomery's bus system. Energized by the court decisions and actions such as the Montgomery boycott, blacks began to launch protests, marches, and other activities designed to secure the rights as citizens that were being denied them.

The most popular and charismatic figure in the civil rights movement was Baptist pastor Martin Luther King Jr. (1929-68), leader of the Montgomery bus boycott. Brought up in a pastor's home, King turned from his religiously conservative upbringing and received his theological training at more liberal schools, Crozer Seminary and Boston University. While in graduate school, King was profoundly influenced by reading American transcendentalist Henry David Thoreau and Hindu political philosopher Mohandas Gandhi. From them, King borrowed the idea of using nonviolent resistance and civil disobedience (refusing to obey laws that one thinks are unjust) in order to achieve social and political change. Knowing the history of black churches in political activism, King became convinced that black churches could serve as the vehicles of such reform in the United States. In 1957 King and his associates organized the Southern Christian Leadership Conference to further the cause of black rights.

King and his supporters held rallies in churches and used the churches as centers for drives to register blacks to vote. Clergymen were in the forefront in August 1963 when over two hundred thousand people—both black and white—gathered in the nation's capital for a march on Washington, the largest civil rights protest in United States history. Speaking in front of the Lincoln Memorial, King told the crowds, "I have a dream that my four little children will one day live in a nation where they will not be judged by the color of their skin but by the content of their character."

Shortly thereafter, under President Johnson's prodding, Congress passed both the Civil Rights Act of 1964 and the Voting Rights Act of 1965. King's assassination in Memphis in 1968 became a kind of martyrdom to his followers, and the churches he had stirred to action continued to involve themselves heavily in politics. One of his assistants, the Reverend Jesse Jackson, ran twice with some success for the Democratic party's nomination for president (1984 and 1988).

Struggles in the Church

The black church could not help being affected by the national controversy over civil rights. A major conflict took place within the National Baptist Convention, U.S.A., Inc., in the early 1960s. Joseph H. Jackson, president of the National Baptist Convention from 1953 to 1982, opposed Martin Luther King's use of civil disobedience to achieve black equality. He argued that blacks should work through the court system for change, and he wanted to try to keep the church out of politics. In addition, some of his opponents viewed his control of the convention as dictatorial. A series of clashes in the national meetings of 1960 and 1961 resulted in a split. The large majority followed Jackson. Martin Luther King and several others formed the Progressive National Baptist Convention. King's new group involved itself much more deeply in the civil rights movement. Jackson himself was finally ousted by those in the National Baptists who wanted to involve the convention more in political activity.

In the 1960s many black political activists became more insistent in their demands for change. An expression of this spirit was "Black Power," a call for securing black rights even by violence if necessary. A religious form of Black Power emerged in black theology. This approach to theology reinterpreted the biblical and traditional black emphasis on freedom almost solely as a political goal of social change. Supernatural salvation of the sinner through the atoning work of Christ received little mention by advocates of black theology as they stressed social and economic reform. Sometimes it seemed to outsiders that the black church was becoming little more than a political action group that used biblical terminology.

Balancing the Equation

Since the 1960s, many of the most prominent black religious leaders, especially in the major black denominations, have proclaimed politically liberal policies of social activism. Furthermore, the church's involvement in the civil rights movement and the publicizing of black theology may give the impression that the black church has been completely radicalized. This is not the case.

African American Christians have become more aware of their heritage and more interested in their history. But not all embrace the tenets of Black Power or downplay the supernatural gospel of the salvation of sinners through Christ. Researchers found in 1990, for example, that only a third of urban black pastors (who tend to be more activist than rural pastors) said they were influenced by black theology (C. Eric Lincoln and Lawrence H. Mamiya, *The Black Church in the African American Experience,* p. 179). In his 1984 address to the First National Assembly of Black Churches, theology professor Gayraud Wilmore said, "Most Black churches believe in a decisive 'born again' experience, reject the historical-critical method of Biblical interpretation, hold to a more or less puritanical prohibition against smoking, drinking, gambling, etc., and embrace many of the tenets of fundamentalism."

In short, the black church as a whole cannot be easily typified. Most churches, but not all, are socially active in seeking black equality. All dream, with Martin Luther King, of a society in which they and their children "will not be judged by the color of their skin but by the content of their character." Some churches are theologically liberal, but it is probable that the majority are doctrinally conservative. And about issues such as drug addiction, divorce, and declining educational standards in the schools, black Christians are certainly no less concerned than white Christians. Indeed, African Americans often understand firsthand the effects of these problems more than the white population does.

One cannot ignore the differences in culture that have separated black and white Christians; the history of those differences is too long. Nor should anyone ignore those differences if it leaves him unaware of the heritage and contributions of the black church in American history. Many African American Christians have demonstrated by their unflinching faith in God the truth of the apostle Paul's words: "For ye are all the children of God by faith in Christ Jesus. For as many of you as have been baptized into Christ have put on Christ. There is neither Jew nor Greek, there is neither bond nor free, there is neither male nor female: for ye are all one in Christ Jesus" (Gal. 3:26-28).

For Further Reading

Boyer, Horace Clarence. *How Sweet the Sound: The Golden Age of Gospel.* Washington, D.C.: Elliott and Clark, 1995.

Clark, Erskine. *Wrestlin' Jacob: A Portrait of Religion in the Old South.* Atlanta: John Knox Press, 1979.

Fitts, Leroy. *A History of Black Baptists.* Nashville: Broadman, 1985.

Lincoln, C. Eric and Lawrence H. Mamiya. *The Black Church in the African American Experience.* Durham, N.C.: Duke University Press, 1990.

Raboteau, Albert J. *Slave Religion: The "Invisible Institution" in the Antebellum South.* New York: Oxford University Press, 1978.

Sernett, Milton C., ed. *Afro-American Religious History: A Documentary Witness.* 2nd ed. Durham, N.C.: Duke University Press, 1999.

———. *Bound for the Promised Land: African American Religion in the Great Migration.* Durham, N.C.: Duke University Press, 1997.

Skinner, Tom. *Black and Free.* Grand Rapids: Zondervan, 1970.

Woodson, Carter. *The History of the Negro Church.* 3rd ed. Washington, D.C.: Associated Publishers, 1921, 1945, 1972.

JOHN MARRANT

In the eighteenth century, America saw its first great revival of religion. The Great Awakening, as it is known, touched lives throughout the American colonies. In New England, pastor-theologian Jonathan Edwards wrote and preached extensively in defense of the revival. His sermon "Sinners in the Hands of an Angry God" is probably the most famous literary product of the awakening. From England came George Whitefield, a powerful evangelist who, with John Wesley, had been used of God to further revival in Great Britain. His preaching tours of the American colonies attracted thousands of hearers and saw countless conversions to Christ. He was an eloquent preacher whose thundering voice God used to melt hearts hardened by sin. American printer and inventor Benjamin Franklin estimated that Whitefield could speak to a crowd of thirty thousand in the open air and still be heard.

God's grace in the Great Awakening knew no limits of class, culture, or race. In that revival historians find the first records of significant numbers of African Americans publicly embracing Christ. As a result, the first independent black churches were born in the latter days of the awakening. Among the many "new creatures in Christ Jesus" saved during the awakening was a convert of Whitefield's, a young black man who enjoyed a varied and dramatic ministry of his own. His name was John Marrant.

EARLY YEARS AND CONVERSION

John Marrant was born in 1755 in New York. His father died when John was four, and his mother moved south, first to St. Augustine, Florida, and later to Georgia. When he was eleven, John's mother sent him to Charleston, South Carolina, to live with his older sister and her husband, where he was to be apprenticed to learn a trade. His career took a detour, however. He recalled, "I had passed by a school, and heard music and dancing, which took my fancy very much, and I felt a strong inclination to learn the music. I went home and informed my sister that I would rather learn to play upon music than go to a trade." His sister sent this news to her mother, who immediately rushed to Charleston to put a stop to the

15

idea. John was stubborn, though, and his mother relented. She sent him to the school, where he learned to play the violin and French horn with great skill. By the age of thirteen, Marrant said, "I was invited to all the balls and assemblies that were held in the town, and met with the general applause of the inhabitants. I was a stranger to want, being supplied with as much money as I had any occasion for."

Having indulged his musical tastes, Marrant finally agreed to be apprenticed. Even then, however, he spent many evenings playing his instruments at parties and dances. Sometimes he stayed out all night, making his work the next day of little profit to his employer.

One evening he was going with a friend to play his horn somewhere when they passed a church thronged about with a large crowd. On being told that "a crazy man was hallooing there," Marrant wanted to enter. His companion agreed to join him only if Marrant would blast on his French horn as the minister was preaching. Marrant shoved his way inside and found that the "crazy man" was Evangelist George Whitefield. Marrant was getting ready to blow his horn when Whitefield announced his text. The evangelist, Marrant thought, looked directly at the young man, pointed his finger at him, and declared, "Prepare to meet thy God, O Israel" (Amos 4:12). At these words, Marrant collapsed. When he came to himself, he heard Whitefield still speaking, and he later recalled that "every word I heard from the minister was like a parcel of swords thrust into me." Weak from conviction of sin, he was taken to the vestry, where Whitefield came to him after the service. He looked at John and said, "Jesus Christ has got thee at last." Since he was leaving Charleston the next day, Whitefield could not visit Marrant at home but promised to send another minister to speak with him.

Marrant was carried home so wrought up with conviction of sin that his sister thought he was dying and sent for doctors. For three days he ate and drank little. On the fourth day came the minister Whitefield had promised, a local Baptist pastor in Charleston. The minister and Marrant knelt together beside the bed and prayed. At the end of the prayer, the minister asked Marrant how he felt.

"Much worse," was the reply.

They prayed again, and the minister said, "How do you do now?"

"Worse and worse," said Marrant.

They prayed a third time. "Near the close of his prayer," Marrant said, "the Lord was pleased to set my soul at liberty, and being filled with joy, I began to praise the Lord immediately. My sorrows were turned into peace, and joy, and love."

"How is it now?" asked the minister.

"All is well, all happy," answered Marrant. Afterwards, the pastor continued to visit the young convert and advised, "Hold fast that thou hast already obtained, till Jesus Christ come."

REJECTION AND FLIGHT

Marrant began reading the Bible hungrily and ignoring his musical instruments. His sister said he was crazy, so after about three weeks he went to see his mother. He stayed with her about five weeks, but his brother and sisters were not sympathetic to the change in his life: "They called me every name but that which was good." Even his mother turned against him. Marrant read his Bible and fasted, but he was miserable to the point of contemplating suicide. Finally Marrant decided to leave home. He was just under fifteen years old.

Marrant's family lived on the frontier of colonial Georgia. Beyond the settlements where they lived was wilderness inhabited only by the Indians. Marrant took off into that wilderness with only "a small pocket Bible and one of Dr. Watts' hymn books." He walked along, reading his Bible, singing hymns, and praying (often aloud). He made do with what little food and water he could find and slept in trees at night for fear of wild animals. For several days, he went on this way, growing weaker from hunger but continuing to pray and to meditate about his Lord. As Marrant passed one tree, an Indian hunter, who had spied Marrant approaching, suddenly reached out and seized him. Having heard Marrant praying aloud, he asked whom he was talking to. When Marrant said "my Lord Jesus," he quickly had to explain to the puzzled hunter that Christ could not be seen.

> He . . . asked me how I did to live. I said I was supported by the Lord. He asked me how I slept. I answered the Lord provided me with a bed every night. He further inquired what preserved me from being devoured by the wild beasts? I replied, the Lord Jesus Christ kept me from them. He stood astonished, and said, "You say the Lord Jesus Christ does this, and does that, and does everything for you; He must be a fine man; where is He?" I replied, "He is here present." To this he made no answer.

To Marrant's surprise, he learned that the hunter knew Marrant's family and at first wanted to take the young man back home. When Marrant objected, the hunter then said that at least Marrant should accompany him as he hunted. Therefore, for a little more than ten weeks he traveled with the hunter, camping with him and helping him to build his camps and to skin the deer he caught. He also began to learn the Cherokee language from the hunter.

AMONG THE INDIANS

After some ten weeks of hunting, the hunter took Marrant with him back to a Cherokee town. There, the Cherokees ignored the hunter's pleas and seized Marrant as an intruder. One of the chiefs examined him. He felt sorry for young Marrant, he said, but he had to die according to their law. Imprisoned overnight and sentenced to die in the morning, Marrant spent the night singing and praying. A guard outside thought someone must be in the prison house with Marrant, and he summoned the executioner. This man dashed in with a torch but found Marrant alone. Asked whom he was talking to, Marrant answered, "The Lord Jesus Christ." The executioner left without saying a word to this strange prisoner.

The time of execution came and Marrant learned for the first time the fate intended for him. "The executioner showed me a basket of turpentine wood stuck full of small pieces like skewers. He told me I was to be stripped naked and laid down in the basket, and these sharp pegs were to be stuck into me, and then set on fire, and when they burnt to my body, I was to be turned on the other side and served in the same manner, and then to be taken by four men and thrown into the flame, which was to finish my execution. I burst into tears, and asked him what I had done to deserve so cruel a death."

Marrant asked permission to pray, which was granted. He began praying in English but then felt moved to pray in Cherokee. Hearing the captive speaking in their own language, the Cherokees listened, and the prayers moved them. When Marrant finished praying, the executioner hugged him and said, "No man shall hurt thee till thou hast been to the king." Marrant fully believed the man had actually been converted, and he prayed in thanksgiving: "What can't the Lord Jesus do, and what power is like unto His? I will thank Thee for what is past, and trust Thee for what is to come. I will sing Thy praise with my feeble tongue whilst life and breath shall last, and when I fail to sound Thy praises here, I hope to sing them round Thy throne above."

The executioner took Marrant back to the chief who had condemned the young man to death and begged that he be taken to the king of the Cherokees. Inside the king's house Marrant told the king how he had met the hunter and how he had come to the town and been arrested. The king asked about Marrant's "Lord Jesus Christ" and was puzzled by the claim that Christ was present but not visible. The king's daughter entered as they conversed and noticed the Bible that Marrant had. The king asked what it was. "I told him that the name of my God was recorded there," said Marrant. Being asked to read, he read Isaiah 53 and Matthew 26. Marrant said that his God had made heaven and earth; the king denied this. "I then pointed to the sun, and asked him who made the sun, and moon, and stars, and preserved them in their regular order. He said that there was a man in their town that did it. I laboured as much as I could to convince him to the contrary."

The king's daughter picked up the Bible, looked at it, and "said with much sorrow the book would not speak to her." The executioner urged the king to have Marrant pray. The effect was not what they expected. As Marrant prayed, several Cherokees in the group came under deep conviction of sin—including the king's daughter. She became so miserable that the king declared Marrant a witch and had him imprisoned again with orders to execute him the next morning. The executioner kept pleading Marrant's case to the king; so the next morning instead of taking the young man to the place of execution, the guards brought him back to the king. Marrant, at the king's request, prayed fervently for his daughter. As a result, the king, the daughter, and several others were converted. Now they embraced Marrant and took him as a guest into the king's house.

John now began to dress like a Cherokee, and he practiced their language until he was quite fluent. After dwelling several weeks with the Cherokees and sharing God's Word with them as best he knew how, Marrant desired to visit the other nearby Indian tribes and tell them of God's love. He spent five weeks with the Creeks, then went to the Catawars, and finally spent seven weeks with the Howsaws. He saw no results from this work—certainly nothing like the dramatic conversions that he had seen among the Cherokees—and he finally returned to the Cherokee town.

RETURN HOME AND SERVICE AT SEA

After two years among the Indians, Marrant desired to see his family once again, and the Cherokees let him go with some regret. He was not the same young man who had wandered into the wilderness many months before. In addition to being older and more mature, Marrant was now dressed in the Indian fashion: "My dress was partly in the Indian style; the skins of wild beasts composed my garments; my head was set out in the savage manner, with a long pendant down my back, a sash round my middle, . . . and a tomahawk by my side." Back among the white settlements, he first came upon a house at dinnertime, and his appearance so frightened the family that they fled. He sat down and ate part of their still-warm meal and then went to look for them. He first found only one child peeking from behind a barn—who fainted when he approached. Finally, all the family returned and, after hearing his story, welcomed him. Marrant stayed six weeks with the family, holding services on Sundays with them and some neighboring families.

Eventually traveling on, Marrant arrived at home and found that his family did not recognize him because of his Indian dress and changed appearance. They had thought him dead, having searched for him and found a dead body, the victim of wild animals, that they thought was his. His wilderness adventures over, Marrant went with his brother to work as a carpenter on a plantation about seventy miles from Charleston. Each night, after finishing his work, Marrant would read his Bible, pray, and sing hymns. His devotions caught the attention of some slave children on the plantation, and he began teaching them the Scripture and helping them memorize the Lord's Prayer. Soon their parents also came so that Marrant was ministering to about thirty slaves.

The mistress of the plantation was enraged when she heard of this activity. She goaded her husband into breaking up the meetings. The master and his assistants not only halted the meetings but also beat all the slaves who had been attending. The mistress wanted her husband to beat Marrant too, be he feared trouble with the law if he beat a free black.

He ended up serving in the American Revolution, but not intentionally. The British, to get crews for the hard life aboard British warships, would "impress" men to serve, that is, seize them and force them into service. Marrant was impressed into the British navy and eventually served just under seven years. Despite the involuntary nature of his service, he seems to have grown used to it. Marrant saw military action, but he also saw reminders of how God had dealt with him in the past. He was with the British forces in 1780 laying siege to Charleston, South Carolina, the scene of his conversion under Whitefield's preaching. When the city fell, he went ashore and was surprised to see the old Cherokee king riding into the city with the British commander, General Henry Clinton. The king greeted Marrant warmly and said that he and his daughter both still enjoyed peace with God.

Marrant became backslidden while in the navy. He said, "With shame [I] confess that a lamentable stupor crept over all my spiritual vivacity, life and vigour; I got cold and dead." God continued to work with Marrant, though. Once during a storm, the sea three times washed him overboard into shark-infested waters and then the action of the waves hurled him back onto the deck. This harrowing, narrow escape from death in the deep jolted him: "These were the means the Lord used to revive me, and I began now to set out afresh."

John Marrant was in at least one major sea battle, the Battle of Dogger Bank in the North Sea against the Dutch on August 5, 1781. He was serving as a cannoneer on the eighty-gun *Princess Amelia,* the most powerful British ship in the force. He described the horror and violence of the clash: "We had a great number killed and wounded; the deck was running with blood; six men were killed and three wounded stationed at the same gun with me. My head and face were covered with the blood and brains of the slain. I was wounded, but did not fall till a quarter of an hour before the engagement ended." Hospitalized for three months, he then served in a convoy to the West Indies but was dismissed from the service on his return to England because of ill health.

RESTORATION AND RENEWED SERVICE

In London, Marrant tried to gather his wages from his service but ran into delays. Being stuck in London without money completed the work of humbling him that God had begun while Marrant was at sea. He eventually went to work for a cotton merchant for three years, but more important he sought God once more. Marrant joined a group known as the Huntington Connexion of the Calvinistic Methodists, whose origins lay in the preaching of none other than George Whitefield, the fiery evangelist who had shown Marrant the way to Christ. The major supporter of the group was a noblewoman, Selina, Countess of Huntington, who gave generously of her money to support the preaching of the gospel. She took a special interest in providing the financial means for ministers to carry out the Lord's work.

As he again joined with other Christians in worship, Marrant found himself beginning once again to minister to others. He began preaching and felt a new impulse as though a voice was crying "Go forth." He testified, "During this time I saw my call to the ministry fuller and clearer; had a feeling concern for the salvation of my countrymen," that is, the blacks of North America. On May 15, 1785, he was ordained to the ministry by the Huntington Connexion. Prior to his ordination, he gave his testimony in great detail. Impressed by the story, fellow minister William Aldridge shaped the testimony into a short pamphlet. *A Narrative of the Life of John Marrant,* edited by Aldridge, was published in 1785 in London. "I . . . wish these gracious dealings of the Lord with me to be published," Marrant said in the opening sentences, "in hopes they may be useful to others; to encourage the fearful, to confirm the wavering, and to refresh the hearts of true believers." What followed was the story of his conversion under Whitefield's preaching, his testimony to the Cherokees, and the other circumstances that had led to his ordination. The little work proved remarkably popular and was reprinted nineteen times over the next forty years.

RETURN TO NORTH AMERICA

Prior to his ordination, Marrant had received a letter from his brother, now in Nova Scotia, Canada. He told John of a colony of blacks in the province and urged him to come and preach to them. Marrant showed the letter to the Countess of Huntington who, after reading it, urged him to go there to minister. With the support of the Huntington Connexion, Marrant left for Nova Scotia. He preached to blacks there and eventually gathered a church of forty in Birch Town. He also preached to the Indians in Canada, entering their wigwams and speaking to them of Christ. For four years he trekked through the Canadian wilderness preaching to blacks, whites, and Indians.

In 1789 Marrant went to Boston, where he preached, sometimes in the face of threats of mob violence. It was there he preached one of his few sermons that have been preserved. In that message he spoke of the equality of all men before God. He condemned those who "despise those they would make, if they could, a species below them, and as not made of the same clay with themselves." Marrant proclaimed the dignity of man as a creation of God and the sin of making false distinctions among humankind:

> Thus man is crowned with glory and honor, he is the most remarkable workmanship of God. And is man such a noble creature and made to converse with his fellow men that are of his own order, to maintain mutual love and society, and to serve God in consort with each other?—then what can these God-provoking wretches think, who despise their fellow

men, as tho' they were not of the same species with themselves, and would if in their power deprive them of the bless-
ings and comforts of this life, which God in His bountiful
goodness hath freely given to all His creatures to improve and
enjoy? Surely such monsters never came out of the hand of
God in such a forlorn condition.

The circumstances that blacks endured, Marrant said, made
them in no way inferior to other races or cultures:

"Ancient history will produce some of the Africans who were
truly good, wise, and learned men, and as eloquent as any
other nation whatever though at present many of them [be] in
slavery, which is not a just cause of our being despised; for if
we search history, we shall not find a nation on earth but has
at some period or other of their existence been in slavery,
from the Jews down to the English nation."

This sermon revealed a polished eloquence that would seem to
promise a bright future to the minister. Marrant's health was apparently bad, however, and he wanted to return to England to see
his friends there. This he did, leaving Boston on February 5, 1790.
He died about a year later and was buried near London. He was but
thirty-six years old. A fitting epitaph, perhaps, is found in one of
his sermons:

Let it be remembered, that all that is outward, whether opinions, rites or ceremonies, cannot be of importance in regard
to eternal salvation. . . . Unhappily, too many Christians, so
called, take their religion not from the declarations of Christ
and his apostles, but from the writings of those they esteem
learned.—But, I am to say, it is from the New Testament only,
not from any books whatsoever, however piously wrote, that
we ought to seek what is the essence of Christ's religion; and
it is from this fountain I have endeavored to give my hearers
the idea of Christianity in its spiritual dress, free from any
human mixtures.

For Further Reading

Potkay, Adam, and Sandra Burr, ed. *Black Atlantic Writers of the 18th
Century.* New York: St. Martin's Press, 1995. Contains the most ac-
curate available version of *A Narrative of the Life of John Marrant*
(Marrant's brief autobiography) and a sermon Marrant preached in
1789 (pp. 67-122).

Saillant, John. "Hymnody and the Persistence of an African-American
Faith in Sierra Leone." *The Hymn*, January 1997, pp. 8-17.

A *pioneer* is someone who launches into the unknown. He might be a settler clearing a wilderness, or he might be a scientist seeking a cure for a deadly disease through a new line of research. In Christian history, a pioneer is one who carries the gospel to an area where the name of Jesus Christ is little known or to a people who are being ignored by the rest of the Christian world. George Liele was a true Christian pioneer. Relatively early in his Christian life, he helped found one of the first black churches in America. Then, forced by necessity to leave his home, he went to Jamaica as a missionary more than ten years before Englishman William Carey launched the modern foreign missions movement.

EARLY YEARS AND CONVERSION

George Liele was born a slave around 1750 in Virginia. Like many slaves, he was separated from his parents when he was young. All he knew about his father from secondhand stories was that the elder Liele had been a deeply religious man.

As a young man, George knew almost nothing of salvation through Christ. "I always had a natural fear of God from my youth," he later wrote, "and was often checked in conscience with thoughts of death, which barred me from many sins and bad company. I knew no other way at that time to hope for salvation but only in the performance of my good works." Henry Sharpe, Liele's owner, was a Baptist deacon, a God-fearing man, and a kind master. When Sharpe moved his family to Burke County, Georgia, around 1770, Liele began attending the white Baptist church with his master. On hearing the gospel preached plainly there, Liele realized that there was no salvation in his "best behaviour and good works." He explained, "I was convinced that I was not in the way to heaven, but in the way to hell." Burdened for five or six months by a sense of conviction of sin, Liele was finally converted in 1773. He testified, "I saw my condemnation in my own heart, and I found no way wherein I could escape the damnation of hell, only through the merits of my dying Lord and Saviour Jesus Christ; which caused me to make intercession with Christ, for the salvation of my poor immortal soul." Then he added, "I requested of my Lord and Master to give me a work, I did not care how mean it was, only to try and see how good I would do it."

First Ministry

The first work that God had for George Liele to do others might have indeed thought "mean," or contemptible—explaining the Scripture to other slaves. His success in that ministry caught the attention of the pastor of his master's church. At the urging of the minister, the church licensed Liele to preach. (Some historians believe that George Liele was the first ordained African American Baptist pastor in America.) Henry Sharpe gave Liele his freedom to allow him to preach without hindrance.

Because historical records are so incomplete and sketchy, there is much debate about when and where the first black church in America was founded. George Liele helped establish in the 1770s what was at least one of the first: the Silver Bluff Baptist Church in South Carolina, across the Savannah River from Augusta, Georgia. This was a "plantation church," one operated on a plantation with the permission of a sympathetic slave owner. Liele also preached even more extensively and with great success in Savannah, Georgia, and the surrounding area. Many future African American Christian leaders were coworkers with Liele or converts under his preaching. Helping to found the Silver Bluff work was David George, who later became a minister in Nova Scotia and the British colony of Sierra Leone in Africa. Among the converts was Andrew Bryan, founder of the First African Baptist Church in Savannah, the first major black church in the South.

During the Revolutionary War the British occupied Savannah. This situation offered little hardship to Liele; his former master was a Loyalist who served as an officer with the British forces. Liele therefore was able to continue his work with little interference. When Henry Sharpe was killed in battle, however, Sharpe's heirs tried to reenslave Liele. The black preacher was jailed, but he quickly won his freedom by producing the papers that showed he was a free man. Nonetheless, the incident made Liele fearful about his future in Georgia. When the British evacuated Savannah at the end of the war, he thought it safer to leave with them. Liele "indentured" himself as servant to a British officer named Colonel Kirkland. This meant that in return for passage for him and his family (as well as some debt that Liele owed Kirkland), Liele would work for the colonel until the amount was repaid. As a result, George Liele left America with his family for Jamaica.

PREACHER IN JAMAICA

Jamaica, the island to which George Liele came, was at that time a British colony. Christopher Columbus had landed on the island in 1494, and it remained a Spanish colony until 1655, when the British took over. The native islanders died out, and the Spanish—and later the British—brought in slaves to work on the island's extensive sugar plantations. As a result, most of the population were of African descent—and most of them were slaves with little knowledge of salvation through Christ.

Liele and his family arrived in Kingston, Jamaica's main city, in 1783. He served the colonel and paid for his indenture. Once his debt was paid, Liele began preaching among the slaves and free blacks, and he formed a church in a private home in September 1784.

Soon the former slave was gathering a large number of listeners to hear the gospel. Liele certainly did not try to entice them with brief services that could be squeezed into the corners of a busy schedule. His church held two services on Sunday, one from 10:00 to 12:00 in the morning and the other from 4:00 to 6:00 in the afternoon. He held hour-long services on Tuesday and Thursday evenings, and the church also organized meetings for smaller groups on Monday evenings. Baptismal services were regular and very public. Every three months, Liele and his church members made a procession through the town to an outdoor site, where they publicly baptized professing converts either in the ocean or in a river. By this practice, converts openly declared their identification with the cause of Christ.

Liele said of himself and his flock, "We hold to live as nigh the scriptures as we possibly can." His congregation certainly reflected the truth of the Scriptures' claim that "not many wise men after the flesh, not many mighty, not many noble, are called" (I Cor. 1:26). The pastor said of his congregation that "the chiefest part of our society are poor illiterate slaves, some living on sugar estates, some on mountains, pens, and other settlements, that have no learning, no not so much as to know a letter in the book."

The poverty of the people became evident when they began constructing a church building in Kingston in 1789. Progress was slow. "The chief part of our congregation are slaves," Liele ex-

26

plained in a letter, "and their owners allow them . . . but three or four bits [around 50 cents] per week for allowance to feed themselves; and out of so small a sum we cannot expect anything that can be of service from them; . . . and the free people in our society are but poor, but they are willing, both free and slaves, to do what they can." The building was finally finished in 1793 with financial help from English Baptists.

The poverty of his congregation also forced Liele to find a means besides the ministry to support himself financially. He farmed, but the income from farming was too irregular and insufficient to take care of his family. Therefore, he also kept a wagon and team of horses so that he and his sons could earn money by hauling goods. Liele lamented that financial pressures often forced him to be "too much entangled with the affairs of the world." He considered this need for supporting himself "a hindrance to the Gospel in one way" but in another way it at least allowed him "to set a good example" by proving that he was not trying to wring an easy living for himself from the poor.

However lacking the church was materially, God prospered the work spiritually. By 1793 Liele had baptized some five hundred converts. He was able to establish congregations in other towns and to recruit other preachers to spread the work. He also established a free school for the children of slaves and free blacks. In April of 1793, a deacon in Liele's church and teacher in his school wrote,

> We have great reason in this island to praise and glorify the Lord, for his goodness and loving kindness in sending his blessed Gospel amongst us by our well-beloved minister, Brother Liele. We were living in slavery to sin and Satan, and the Lord hath redeemed our souls to a state of happiness to praise his glorious and ever blessed name; and we hope to enjoy everlasting peace by the promise of our Lord and Master Jesus Christ. The blessed Gospel is spreading wonderfully in this island: believers are daily coming into the church.

OPPOSITION AND PERSECUTION

Liele tried to keep from offending the whites in Jamaica by allowing in his congregation only slaves who had their masters' permission to attend. His church covenant explicitly said, "We permit no slaves to join the church without first having a few lines from their owners of their good behavior." In fact, some modern black writers criticize him, or at least question his wisdom, because of these attempts to accommodate slavery. He should have opposed that institution, they argue, as part of his proclamation of the gospel. Liele apparently did not think so, but despite his caution many whites opposed him. Some white masters thought that blacks were like animals, having no souls, and that therefore preaching to them was useless. Others feared that their slaves might become more troublesome if they became religious or that they might use church meetings to plot rebellions. In 1791 Liele reported, "The people at first persecuted us, both at meeting and baptisms, but God be praised, they seldom interrupt us now." Little did he know what was yet to come.

Beginning in the late 1790s, persecution came in waves. Sometimes the opposition was simply petty harassment. On one occasion, as Liele's congregation was about to partake of the Lord's Supper, a white man rode his horse directly into the church. "Come, old Liele," he said, "give my horse the Sacrament!" Staring the intruder down, Liele replied, "No, Sir, you are not fit yourself to receive it." The pastor in his pulpit faced the mounted rider as several uneasy moments passed until the arrogant trespasser finally turned his horse and left.

Then Liele was jailed in 1797, falsely charged with encouraging rebellion through his preaching. The courts acquitted him, but he was immediately jailed again for almost three and a half years for a debt owed to the builder of his church. (Liele had paid much of the cost of the building himself and was legally responsible for its debts.) He remained in prison until the debt was paid, although we do not know how he or his friends raised the money. While in jail, Liele continued to minister to others. He preached to the other prisoners and gave the Lord's Supper to other Christians in prison. His church continued to function in his absence under the leadership of his son and the deacons of the church. But it also suffered through a lawsuit initiated by one of the deacons, a suit that ended in a split in the church.

After Liele's imprisonment, the persecution became fiercer and more widespread. There was a harsh crackdown on preaching to slaves. Anyone who preached to slaves without legal approval was subject to imprisonment. Slaves found guilty of preaching illegally were subject to whipping. One man reportedly was hanged for the "crimes" of preaching to slaves and baptizing them. Outside the law, vicious gangs attempted to break up black services.

One of the worst atrocities occurred not directly under Liele's ministry but under the ministry of one of his converts and fellow preachers, Moses Hall. Determined to put an end to slave meetings, some slave owners broke up a prayer meeting being led by a slave named David, one of Hall's assistants. They seized David, murdered him, cut off his head, and placed it on a pole in the center of the village as a warning to the other slaves. They dragged Moses Hall up to the grisly object.

"Now, Moses Hall, whose head is that?" the leader of the murderers asked.

"David's," Moses replied.

"Do you know why he is up here?"

"For praying, Sir," said Moses.

"No more of your prayer meetings," he said. "If we catch you at it, we shall serve you as we have served David."

As the crowd watched, Moses knelt beside the pole and said, "Let us pray." The other blacks gathered around and knelt with him as he prayed for the salvation of the murderers. Astounded, the slave owners departed, leaving Moses and his followers unharmed.

FINAL YEARS

We have little record of Liele's later ministry. We know that between 1801, the end of his imprisonment, and 1810 he conducted work in the interior of Jamaica, establishing churches there. That would seem to be the pattern of his final years: ministering to the works he had established and establishing new works wherever he could. Liele died in 1828. His pioneer work in Jamaica was fruitful. Baptists were a small and struggling sect in Jamaica when he came. By 1814 they numbered eight thousand, and within five years of his death they totaled over twenty thousand. Obviously, George Liele was not responsible for all of this growth by himself. For one thing, other faithful preachers—many of whom Liele had pointed to Christ—shared in the work. Above all, it was the blessing of God's Spirit upon George Liele and the others that brought thousands to salvation. The God who calls "not many wise men after the flesh, not many mighty, not many noble" is the one who "hath chosen the foolish things of the world to confound the wise; and . . . the weak things of the world to confound the things which are mighty."

For Further Reading

Davis, John W. "George Liele and Andrew Bryan, Pioneer Negro Baptist Preachers." *Journal of Negro History* 3 (1918): 119-27.

Holmes, E. A. "George Liele: Negro Slavery's Prophet of Deliverance." *Baptist Quarterly* 20 (1964): 340-51, 361.

Rusling, G. W. "A Note on Early Negro Baptist History." *Foundations* 11 (1968): 362-68.

Sernett, Milton. "The Expatriate Option." *Christian History*, vol. 18, no. 2, 1999.

Methodism came to America about the time of the War for Independence. The Methodist movement had been born in England under the leadership of John Wesley (1703-91), his brother Charles (1707-88), and several other outstanding men of faith. The individual most responsible for helping Methodism get started in North America was Bishop Francis Asbury (1745-1816). He developed one of the distinctive institutions of American Methodism: circuit riding. Dividing the land into sections, or "circuits," a circuit rider would travel on horseback from town to town and from settlement to settlement preaching the good news of salvation in Christ. Nothing seemed to stop these hardy pioneers of the gospel. Frontier settlers had a saying about bad weather: "There is nothing out today but crows and Methodist preachers."

Although Methodism proved successful in reaching all classes of people, it had a particular appeal to the downtrodden. Methodist preachers presented the gospel in sincere simplicity to "*every* creature." Because of this universal approach and also because of early Methodism's opposition to slavery, African Americans flocked to the denomination. Soon only the Baptists could claim more black members. One of the most important black leaders in Methodist history was Richard Allen, founder of the most important black Methodist denomination, the African Methodist Episcopal Church.

EARLY YEARS, CONVERSION, AND FREEDOM

Richard Allen was born a slave on February 14, 1760, in Philadelphia. In 1768 he was sold with his family to planter Stokeley Sturgis who lived near Dover, Delaware. Allen's master was not a Christian, but he was "affectionate and tender-hearted," Allen said, "what the world called a good master." Unfortunately, Sturgis was also hard pressed financially. Somewhere around 1776, debts forced Sturgis to sell Allen's mother along with three of her children; Allen and one brother and one sister remained with Sturgis.

This wrenching event must have affected Allen deeply. He found comfort a year or so later, though, when he heard the gospel. Allen recalled, "I was awakened and brought to see myself, poor, wretched and undone, and without the mercy of God must be lost.

Shortly after, I obtained mercy through the blood of Christ." Immediately afterwards, however, he went through a period of doubting:

> I was brought under doubts, and was tempted to believe I was deceived, and was constrained to seek the Lord afresh. I went with my head bowed down for many days. My sins were a heavy burden. I was tempted to believe there was no mercy for me. I cried to the Lord both night and day. One night I thought hell would be my portion. I cried unto Him who delighteth to hear the prayers of a poor sinner, and all of a sudden my dungeon shook, my chains flew off, and, glory to God, I cried. My soul was filled. I cried, enough for me—the Saviour died. Now my confidence was strengthened that the Lord, for Christ's sake, had heard my prayers and pardoned all my sins. I was constrained to go from house to house, exhorting my old companions, and telling to all around what a dear Saviour I had found.

Allen, his brother, and his sister were all converted. Neighbors scoffed that Sturgis's slaves would be of little use to him now that they had "got religion." Allen knew of the doubters, so he and his brother "held a council together, that we would attend more faithfully to our master's business, so that it should not be said that religion made us worse servants."

The change in Allen and his brother so impressed Sturgis that the planter asked Allen to have the Methodist preacher to come speak to him. After hearing the gospel, Sturgis was also converted. Furthermore, he embraced the Methodist opposition to slavery. The planter wanted to free his slaves, but he was in debt and could not easily do so. Therefore, he decided to let Allen and his brother earn the money to purchase their liberty. Sturgis released them in 1780, but they were still officially the planter's slaves until they paid for their freedom. Allen immediately set to work, but it was hard, for all Allen was qualified to do was manual labor. He recalled that after chopping wood for a full day "my hands were so blistered and sore, that it was with difficulty I could open or shut them." He also worked in a brickyard and as a teamster, hauling goods in a horse-drawn wagon. Nagging at him too was the fact that the aging Sturgis might die before all the payments were made. Allen had no idea what might happen to him then. But in three years, Richard Allen paid the money, and he was a free man. "I had it often impressed upon my mind that I should one day enjoy my freedom," Allen wrote. "For slavery is a bitter pill, notwithstanding we had a good master."

METHODIST PREACHER

Even as a slave, Richard Allen had spoken to other slaves concerning their need of salvation in Christ. While working for his freedom, he devoted evenings and Sundays to preaching, wherever he had opportunity. "Sometimes," Allen recalled, "I would awake from my sleep, preaching and praying." After he had purchased his liberty, Allen began to preach more regularly for the Methodists. Instead of being a circuit rider, Allen was more of a "circuit walker," traveling on foot to his preaching engagements. He recalled one of his early preaching tours: "I walked until my feet became so sore and blistered the first day, that I scarcely could bear them to the ground." He stopped for the night with a friendly couple and could not even bear to walk to the table for supper. Therefore they carried the table to him and helped him soak his feet all night to relieve the pain. He stayed with them through Sunday preaching, when he preached with such effect that he remained several weeks and saw many sinners converted.

Alternating working and preaching was his pattern: "My usual method was, when I would get bare of clothes, to stop travelling and go to work. . . . My hands administered to my necessities." A brief testimonial about his work from 1780 to 1786 says that "he Traveled into various parts of New York, New Jersey, Pensilva., Delaware, Virginia, Maryland, and North and South Carolina; and also spent about two Months in visiting the Indian natives."

Only a few scattered records describe his early ministry. A testimonial notes that in Delaware Allen found a trunk filled with silver and gold. He advertised in the papers and eventually found the owner. When the relieved man tried to give Allen a cash reward, he refused, "believing it to be wrong to accept of such Rewards." Then the owner tried to get Allen to take a new suit made of the finest materials, but again Allen refused. Finally the preacher accepted a suit of coarse cloth from the grateful owner.

Allen also became an acquaintance of Bishop Francis Asbury. They may have met first in 1779 when the bishop had visited the Sturgis farm and preached there while Allen was still a slave. After Allen was free, Asbury invited him to travel with him and to preach. Such an evangelistic team was not unusual for Asbury; he had conducted preaching tours with African American Harry Hosier (popularly called "Black Harry"), who had proved a powerfully effective preacher. Now Asbury was inviting Allen to join him for a tour, including trips to the South. Asbury was honest with Allen. He said that in the South Allen "must not intermix with the slaves, and . . . would frequently have to sleep in his carriage." Furthermore, he would receive (like Asbury) no pay outside of his food and shelter. Allen respected the bishop, but he refused to go under these conditions. He told Asbury that he believed that while he was young and healthy, he must devote at least part of his efforts to working and saving for retirement or sudden illness. The respected and well-loved Bishop Asbury, Allen said, could reasonably expect others to care for him in case of illness or old age. Allen was not at all convinced that anyone would do the same for him. Asbury bore no grudges for this refusal and continued to help Allen in his ministry.

In 1786 Richard Allen arrived in Philadelphia. There he began a flourishing work among the city's black population in connection with St. George's Methodist Church. This congregation was the "Mother Church of American Methodism," the first large, established Methodist work in America. Allen and another black preacher, Absalom Jones, worked throughout the week with the blacks of Philadelphia. Then on Sunday mornings the black members joined the white members for the regular worship service. Because of the work of Allen, Jones, and others, the number of African Americans attending St. George's grew—and so did tension with the white majority. Open conflict finally erupted over seating. Originally the black members sat more or less together on the main floor. After a remodeling of the church, they were told to go to the balcony. Allen and the others went, but they apparently went to the "wrong" part of the balcony. During prayer, one of the trustees began pulling Absalom Jones from his knees, saying, "You must get up—you must not kneel here." Jones asked him to wait until prayer was over, but the trustee said, "No, you must get up now, or I will call for aid and force you away." During all this wrangling, the prayer ended. Allen recorded, "We all went out of the church in a body, and they were no more plagued with us in the church."

AN INDEPENDENT CHURCH

Leaving St. George's was an obvious move. But where were the members to go? The bad treatment they had received convinced many that they wanted nothing more to do with the Methodists. Absalom Jones became leader of this group, and they joined the Episcopal Church. Jones became their minister. Allen, however, could not follow them. He wrote, "I was confident that there was no religious sect or denomination would suit the capacity of the colored people as well as the Methodist; for the plain and simple gospel suits best for any people; the unlearned can understand, and the learned are sure to understand." When offered the pastorate of a non-Methodist black church, Allen recorded, "I told them I could not accept of their offer, as I was a Methodist. I was indebted to the Methodists, under God, for what little religion I had; . . . I informed them that I could not be anything else but a Methodist, as I was born and awakened under them."

Allen's first plan was to build a black Methodist church still connected to the Methodist denomination. A small group with Allen as leader began meeting in a rented storeroom. Some white friends donated funds generously to support the work. Allen bought an old blacksmith's shop and then had the building moved to a lot he had purchased. He called his church "Bethel" ("house of God") in prayerful hope that it would be a place where the Lord would dwell and meet with His people. The new Bethel Church was dedicated on June 29, 1794, with Bishop Francis Asbury preaching. Five years later, Asbury ordained Allen. The congregation eventually grew to number thousands.

Despite Asbury's support for Allen and his church, other Methodist leaders did everything they could short of expelling Allen's group in order to bring them under denominational control. Indeed, the leaders sometimes threatened expulsion, to which Allen replied, "If you deny us your name, you cannot seal up the scriptures from us, and deny us a name in heaven. We believe heaven is free for all who worship in spirit and truth." The trustees of Bethel Church issued a statement in 1807 saying, "Our only design is to secure to ourselves, our rights and privileges to regulate our affairs temporal and spiritual, the same as if we were white people, and to guard against any oppression which might possibly arise from the improper prejudices or administration of any individual having the exercise of Discipline over us."

The denominational leaders in Philadelphia tried threats, pleadings, and even trickery to gain control of Bethel. One Methodist leader offered to draw up papers of incorporation for the new church. The congregation agreed, only to find that he had taken advantage of their inexperience and assigned the property to the Methodist denomination. The result was years of legal complications. Another leader trying to assert his authority over the church announced that one Sunday he would come and take charge of the pulpit. The congregation halted him simply by standing in the aisles so that he could not reach the front of the church.

Finally, the church gained legal recognition of its independence in 1816, after years of struggle. In the meantime, Allen had become aware of other black Methodist congregations that had become independent because of discrimination. On April 9, 1816, five of these churches, led by Allen's congregation in Philadelphia and another in Baltimore under the Reverend Daniel Coker, united to form the African Methodist Episcopal (AME) Church. Richard Allen was elected the denomination's first bishop.

Historian Carol George calls the original secession from St. George's and the formation of the AME Church in 1816 "the beginning of the independent black church movement." Actually, independent black churches had emerged earlier in the South. Black Baptists, led by men such as George Liele, David George, and Andrew Bryan, had started independent works in lower South Carolina and coastal Georgia in and around Savannah. But these and other works faced constant legal pressure and racial prejudice. After Nat Turner's slave revolt in Virginia in 1831, restrictions on black churches became so tight that many independent black churches were forced to close. Allen and his followers also faced trials and prejudice in the North, of course, but their work not only endured but also grew.

Allen, however, was not able to unite all of the black Methodists in the North. Many blacks chose to remain within the Methodist Episcopal Church. The AME Church discussed the possibility of a merger with African Methodist Episcopal Zion (AMEZ) Church, a group with a similar name but a different origin. It too had been born when blacks left Methodist churches in New York City over racial discrimination and had been officially organized in the 1820s. Allen suggested uniting the two groups, but many in the AMEZ Church opposed the idea of a union. They accused Allen of trying to build his own little empire by adding their numbers to his group. On one occasion Allen spoke to an AMEZ congregation in an attempt to promote the union of the two groups. One opponent, however, "jumped out of the gallery into the pulpit and sit upon the puliptt [sic] along of Rev. Richard Allen during the time of worship and disturbed the congregation very much. He spit several times on the Rev. Allen while preaching." As a result of this opposition, the two denominations have remained separate works.

MINISTRY TO A CITY

In "A Short Address to the Friends of Him Who Hath No Helper," Richard Allen outlined his priorities in ministering for Christ: "Our Saviour's first and great work was that of the salvation of men's souls; yet we find that of the multitudes who came or were brought to Him laboring under sickness and disorders, He never omitted one opportunity of doing good to their bodies, or sent away one that applied to Him without a perfect cure; though sometimes, for the trial of their faith, He suffered Himself to be importuned." Allen never ignored evangelization, but he also sought to "do good unto all men, especially unto them who are of the household of faith" (Gal. 6:10).

Few incidents illustrate his compassion better than the service he performed during a yellow fever epidemic in Philadelphia in 1793. Many people were sick and dying from the disease, and hundreds fled the city. Philadelphia officials asked Allen and Absalom Jones whether the black community could help relieve the suffering by serving as nurses and by burying the dead. (Part of the reason for asking for black help was the false belief that blacks, being originally from tropical regions, were less susceptible to the disease.) Scores of selfless black men and women, including Allen and Jones themselves, served in the stricken city nursing the sick.

Then, after the epidemic was over, a writer (who had himself fled the city during the epidemic) published an attack on the black workers. He accused them of charging enormous prices for their services and robbing the sick and the dead. Allen and Jones published a response. Black men and women had gone forward in this dangerous work of ministry, they said, "confiding in Him who can preserve in the midst of a burning, fiery furnace." They admitted that some people had charged high prices and that some had been guilty of theft. But not all of these offenders were black. Above all, many black Philadelphians had engaged in brave works of selfless service. Jones and Allen related several such incidents:

> A poor, afflicted, dying man stood at his chamber window, praying and beseeching every one that passed by to help him to a drink of water. A number of white people passed, and instead of being moved by the poor man's distress, they hurried, as fast as they could, out of the sound of his cries, until at length a gentleman, who seemed to be a foreigner, came up. He could not pass by, but had not resolution enough to go into the house. He held eight dollars in his hand, and offered it to several as a reward for giving the poor man a drink of water,

but was refused by every one, until a poor colored man came up. The gentleman offered the eight dollars to him, if he would relieve the poor man with a little water. "Master," replied the good-natured fellow, "I will supply the gentleman with water, but surely I will not take your money for it." . . . He went in, supplied the poor object with water, and rendered him every service he could.

They described other emotionally wrenching scenes. A burial party found a child alone with a corpse, saying, "Mamma is asleep—don't wake her!" Sometimes they entered houses to find nothing but corpses, "some lying on the floor, as bloody as if they had been dipped in it." Death hovered over the city, taking both those who helped and those who hindered: "A white man threatened to shoot us, if we passed by his house with a corpse. We buried him three days after."

In the face of what Philadelphia's black community had done, Allen and Jones felt justified in writing, "We feel ourselves sensibly aggrieved by the censorious epithets of many who did not render the least assistance in the time of necessity, yet are liberal of their censure of us, for the prices paid for our services." The result was nonetheless worth the effort: "This has been no small satisfaction to us; for we think that when a physician was not attainable, we have been the instruments in the hands of God, for saving the lives of some hundreds of our suffering fellow mortals."

STAND FOR FREEDOM

One day after living many years in Philadelphia, Allen was confronted on the street by a man who accused him of being a runaway slave. The man was a professional slave catcher, one who made his living tracking down escaped slaves and turning them in for the reward. Perhaps the slave catcher was simply mistaken or perhaps he, as some in his profession did, hoped to seize some unsuspecting black man unable to defend himself and collect a reward. If it was a plot, it backfired disastrously. Allen easily proved his identity, and the man was imprisoned. Yet the incident was another reminder of how slavery in America affected even free blacks in the North.

Richard Allen was hardly a radical, but he nonetheless wholeheartedly opposed slavery. In "An Address to Those Who Keep Slaves and Approve the Practice," he said, "I do not wish to make you angry, but excite your attention to consider how hateful slavery is in the sight of that God who hath destroyed kings and princes for their oppression of the poor slaves. Pharaoh and his princes, with the posterity of King Saul, were destroyed by the protector and avenger of slaves." He urged them, "If you love your children, if you love your country, if you love the God of love, clear your hands from slaves; burthen not your children or your country with them."

In a parallel address, "To People of Color," he called on those still in slavery to have hope that they might someday be freed as he was. Allen encouraged them to "put your trust in God, who sees your condition, and as a merciful father pitieth his children, so doth God pity them that love Him." He called for them to love their masters and to serve them—with the hope that this behavior might eventually lead to freedom. Even if the masters are cruel in the face of love, "you will have the love and favor of God dwelling in your hearts, which you value more than anything else, which will be a consolation in the worst condition you can be in, and no master can deprive you of it." And if freedom never came, "if the troubles of your condition end with your lives, you will be admitted to the freedom which God hath prepared for those of all colors that love him. Here the power of the most cruel master ends, and all sorrow and tears are wiped away."

To those blacks who were, like him, freed from slavery, he urged no hatred of former masters, saying that God would not approve of hatred in their hearts any more than He did in the children of Israel. He called for the most upright conduct from free blacks—"If we are lazy and idle, the enemies of freedom plead it as a cause why we ought not to be free, and say we are better in a state of servitude; . . . and by such conduct we strengthen the bands of oppression and keep many in bondage who are more worthy than ourselves." Allen called on the freed blacks to consider this situation. "Will even our friends excuse—will God pardon us—for the part we act in making strong the hands of the enemies of our color?"

He was in many ways mild, gentle, and beseeching in his public pronouncements on slavery. But Allen clearly opposed it and sought to combat not only slavery but also every movement that threatened the dignity and security of African Americans. A good example is his battle against the colonization movement. As Americans struggled with the issue of slavery, some well-meaning reformers hit upon the idea of establishing colonies in Africa. Then the blacks could be sent back to Africa, and the problem resolved. Some black preachers, such as Baptist Lott Carey and the AME

Church's own Daniel Coker, even used the support of the colonization movement to establish mission works in Africa.

Allen and other blacks did not oppose mission work by any means. In fact, they did not oppose the idea of colonization so much as the threat it represented. Allen actually approved of plans for colonies for blacks in Canada. But he and others feared that the African colonization movement was aimed more at eliminating free blacks from America's shores than at eliminating slavery. Their suspicions seemed confirmed by the public pronouncements of some advocates of colonization. Slaveholder and statesman Henry Clay, for example, described the nation's free blacks as a "useless and pernicious, if not a dangerous portion of its population." Blacks had no desire to go back to Africa. Allen said in a letter to a newspaper, "This land which we have watered with our tears and our blood, is now our mother country, and we are well satisfied to stay where wisdom abounds and the gospel is free."

In January 1817, three thousand people packed Bethel Church to protest the colonization movement. Allen proudly signed his name to a series of resolutions that the protestors published. Part of this document read as follows:

> *Resolved,* That we never will separate ourselves voluntarily from the slave population in this country; they are our brethren by the ties of consanguinity, of suffering, and of wrongs; and we feel that there is more virtue in suffering privations with them, than fancied advantages for a season.

> *Resolved,* That without arts, without science, without a proper knowledge of Government, to cast into the savage wilds of Africa, the free People of Colour, seems to us a circuitous route to return them to perpetual bondage.

> *Resolved,* That having the strongest confidence in the justice of God, and philanthropy of the free states, we cheerfully submit our destinies to the guidance of Him who suffers not a sparrow to fall without his special Providence.

This assembly to protest colonization was a forerunner of an important force in African American history: the convention movement. Allen was even closer to the events that actually gave birth to the movement. During the early nineteenth century, the state of Ohio saw a large immigration of blacks into its boundaries, and several AME congregations were founded there. Then in 1828 Ohio began requiring every black in state to make a $500 deposit as a guarantee of his or her good behavior. Most blacks, of course, did not have that much money to spare and had to leave the state. Many went to Canada, and the AME churches that had been growing in Ohio were transplanted to Canada. The effect of Ohio's action on Allen's flock caused deep concern within the AME Church. Allen joined in a preliminary meeting in 1830 that issued a call for a meeting in Philadelphia in 1831 to discuss not only this action but also all of the discriminatory policies that black Americans faced. This meeting in Philadelphia in 1831 launched the convention movement. Year after year in city after city, conventions of concerned blacks and sympathetic whites called for advancement for blacks in education, for full citizenship rights for all Americans regardless of color, and above all for the abolition of slavery. Some of the leading African American spokesmen of the era used the convention movement to broadcast their views.

Richard Allen saw none of this. He died on March 26, 1831, shortly before the Philadelphia Convention convened. He had served his city and his race. But he served with a sense of obligation and devotion to God. In a meditation written years before his death, Allen said, "Let my last breath, when my soul shall leave my body, breathe forth love to Thee, my God; I entered into life without acknowledging Thee, let me therefore finish it in loving Thee; O let the last act of life be love, remembering that God is love."

For Further Reading

Allen, Richard. *The Life Experience and Gospel Labors of the Rt. Rev. Richard Allen.* New York: Abingdon, 1960.

George, Carol V. R. *Segregated Sabbaths.* New York: Oxford University Press, 1973.

Gravely, Will. "You Must Not Kneel Here." *Christian History*, vol. 18, no. 2, 1999, pp. 34-36.

Klots, Steve. *Richard Allen: Religious Leader and Social Activist.* New York: Chelsea House Publishers, 1991.

Although Jamestown, Virginia, was the first permanent English settlement in North America, it was New England that most shaped early American character. The Pilgrims of Plymouth Colony and then the Puritans of Massachusetts Bay brought with them a vision. They desired to build a holy commonwealth, a new community dedicated to God and governed by His Word. The churches of New England, dominantly Congregationalist, continued to shape the religious life of America well into the nineteenth century. Congregationalist schools, preachers, and theologians were the pacesetters in American theology. Many important Christian leaders emerged from Congregationalism, such as Jonathan Edwards, pastor-theologian of Massachusetts; Timothy Dwight, president of Yale and leader of revivals in that school; and Asahel Nettleton, America's most important evangelist between George Whitefield and Charles Finney. One member of the Congregationalist "standing order" was an African American, apparently the first black pastor of a white congregation. He was Lemuel Haynes, a man whose career and contribution were indeed unique in American history.

EARLY YEARS

Lemuel Haynes was born July 18, 1753, in West Hartford, Connecticut. A contemporary of Haynes wrote that the child was born into "not only extreme poverty, but the worst kind of orphanage." He was the illegitimate offspring of a black man and a white woman. His mother abandoned him, and he was named not for his parents but for the man in whose house he was born. We know virtually nothing of his parents. Accounts of his mother's identity vary widely. Some sources say she was an immigrant Scottish servant; others say she was from a "respectable" New England family. Of his father even less is known.

At the age of five months, Lemuel was indentured as a servant until he reached the age of twenty-one. Providentially, the family in which he became a servant—that of David Rose of Granville, Massachusetts—was a godly one. Rose was a deacon who had been touched by the Great Awakening, America's first great revival of religion. Haynes recalled his master as a man "of singular piety." Of Mrs. Rose, he had even fonder memories: "His wife, my mistress, had peculiar attachment to me: she treated me as though I was her own child."

Young Lemuel had to work hard, but no harder than the rest of the Rose family there on colonial New England's frontier. The Roses sent him to school, as much as he could be spared, and he also read and studied on his own by firelight in the early morning and late evening. Much of his early learning came from reading a spelling book, the Bible, and a hymnbook.

Haynes loved the Roses as family, and he listened as they taught him of Christ and the Scripture. One incident in his youth that could have diverted Haynes from Christ actually served to show him the importance of the Christian faith. While working for the Roses, when he was about nine or ten years old, Lemuel was much impressed by an irreligious neighbor. The man seemed intelligent, self-assured, and independent. This self-possessed gentleman dismissed the importance of religion and caused Lemuel to question the value of faith. Then the man fell ill, and he hurriedly asked "Deacon Rose" to come pray for him. From this Haynes concluded, "If prayer and religion are needful in sickness and in death, they must be important in health and in life."

It must have been shortly after this that Lemuel Haynes came under a burden of conviction of sin. He described that conviction and his resulting conversion:

> I remember I often had serious impressions, or fearful apprehensions of going to hell. I spent much time in what I called secret prayer. I was one evening greatly alarmed by the *Aurora Borealis,* or *Northern Lights.* It was in that day esteemed a presage of the day of judgment. For many days and nights I was greatly alarmed, through fear of appearing before the bar of God, knowing that I was a sinner; I cannot express the terrors of mind that I felt. One evening, being under an apple-tree mourning my wretched situation, . . . I found the Saviour. I always visit the place when I come to Granville, and, when I can, I pluck some fruit from the tree and carry it home: it is sweet to my taste.

For Lemuel Haynes, prayer and religion would now be needful in health and in life, and years later he would find it sustained him in sickness and in death.

FIGHTING FOR LIBERTY

Throughout his life, Lemuel Haynes was a warrior for the cause of liberty. The American Revolution broke out while he was still living with the Rose family. Haynes enlisted as a minuteman in 1774 and served with General Washington's forces at the siege of Boston in 1775. In 1776 Haynes was a part of the garrison at Fort Ticonderoga in New York, which the Patriots had captured from the British only the year before.

As one who risked his own blood for American liberty, Haynes plainly saw the inconsistency of the American colonies conducting a fight for liberty while leaving millions of blacks in slavery. In a Fourth of July address given in 1801 (the twenty-fifth anniversary of the signing of the Declaration of Independence), he spoke of "the poor Africans," saying, "What has reduced them to their present pitiful, abject state? Is it any distinction that the God of nature hath made in their formation? Nay—but being subjected to slavery, by the cruel hands of oppressors, they have been taught to view themselves as a rank of beings far below others, which has suppressed in a degree, every principle of manhood, and so they become despised, ignorant, and licentious. This shows the effects of despotism and should fill us with the utmost detestation against every attack on the rights of men."

For many years some historians, civil rights activists, and other critics blamed Haynes for not saying more about the issue of slavery. Then in the 1980s historian Ruth Bogin discovered "Liberty Further Extended," an unpublished manuscript by Haynes, written during the American Revolution. In that work, he demonstrated that he was not unconcerned about slavery and that his righteous indignation burned hot against the mistreatment of his race.

Haynes began by quoting now-familiar words from the recently signed Declaration of Independence: "We hold these truths to be self-evident, that all men are created equal, that they are endowed by their Creator with certain unalienable rights, that among these are life, liberty and the pursuit of happiness." With that statement as his starting point, Haynes said,

> We live in a day wherein *liberty and freedom* is the subject of many millions' concern; and the important struggle hath already caused great effusion of blood; men seem to manifest the most sanguine resolution not to let their natural rights go without their lives go with them; a resolution, one would think everyone that has the least love to his country, or future posterity, would fully confide in; yet while we are so zealous

to maintain, and foster our own invaded rights, it cannot be tho't impertinent for us candidly to reflect on our own conduct, and I doubt not but that we shall find subsisting in the midst of us [what] may with propriety be styled *Oppression,* nay, much greater oppression, than that which Englishmen seem so much to spurn at. I mean an oppression which they, themselves, impose upon others.

Leaving no doubt of his position, Haynes wrote, *"a Negro may justly challenge, and has an undeniable right to his liberty: Consequently, the practice of slave-keeping, which so much abounds in this land, is illicit."*

Haynes did not limit his arguments to the Declaration of Independence. Quoting Acts 17:26, "And [God] hath made of one blood all nations of men for to dwell on all the face of the earth, and hath determined the times before appointed, and the bounds of their habitation," Haynes said that "all are of one species" and that therefore all men enjoy the same natural rights, including the right to liberty. "Liberty," wrote Haynes, "is equally as precious to a *black man,* as it is to a *white one,* and bondage equally intolerable to the one as it is to the other." Under the blessing and gift of God, black men should enjoy liberty just as white men. "God has been pleas'd to distinguish some men from others, as to natural abilities, but not as to natural *right,* as they came out of his hands."

Haynes had even stronger words for the cruel slave trade: "O! what an immense deal of African blood hath been Shed by the inhuman cruelty of Englishmen! that reside in a Christian Land! . . . O ye that have made yourselves drunk with human Blood! altho' you may go with impunity here in the life, yet God will hear the cries of that innocent blood, which cries from the sea, and from the ground against you, like the blood of Abel." Slavery he called simply "a hell upon Earth; and all this for filthy lucre's sake." Haynes never personally experienced the degradation of slavery, but that fact did not keep him from protesting against it.

ENTERING THE MINISTRY

After he turned twenty-one and his indenture was ended, Haynes continued to live with the Roses. He continued his private study, turning more to the study of theology. How well he had learned this new subject was revealed in an unusual manner. Often in the Rose family devotions, one member of the circle would read a published sermon by some famous preacher. One Saturday night Haynes read a sermon based on John 3:3, "Verily, verily, I say unto thee, Except a man be born again, he cannot see the kingdom of God." Afterwards, Mr. Rose observed that it was a very good sermon and asked, "Lemuel, whose work is that which you have been reading? Is it Davies's sermon, or Watts's, or Whitefield's?" Haynes replied sheepishly, "It's Lemuel's sermon." He had slipped in one that he had written himself from his own study. The maturity of the work astonished not only Rose but also others who read it. Increasingly, their church in Granville called upon Haynes to help in the work, such as reading other people's sermons in the absence of a regular speaker.

The writing of this sermon was the first public display of Lemuel Haynes's interest in the Christian ministry. Haynes, with his irregular education and poor social background, was fearful of attending college. However, it was common at that time for a candidate for the ministry to study under individual pastors, and Haynes eagerly launched into such study. Although such preparation was "informal," it was far from easy or superficial. From each pastor/teacher, he learned some aspect of the Christian ministry. For example, he worked as a schoolteacher in exchange for his room, board, and tuition while one pastor taught him Greek. Haynes became very proficient in the Greek New Testament and in the Septuagint (the Greek translation of the Old Testament). The Reverend Mr. Daniel Farrand helped Haynes with homiletics, the preparation and delivery of sermons. Farrand was a man who knew how to keep the practical in focus. After listening to Lemuel give a trial sermon filled with eloquent, elevated terminology, Farrand said, "Mr. Haynes, you have been talking, it seems by your style, to the inhabitants of the upper world; what if you should come down to folks on the earth, so that we can understand you?"

At the age of twenty-seven, Haynes began his first ministry as a pulpit supply (a kind of interim pastor) in a newly formed church in Middle Granville, Massachusetts. He spent five years there and saw both the conversion of sinners and the spiritual growth of saints. One of those converts became especially important to him. She was Elizabeth Babbit, a schoolteacher. Not only did she become a member of the church, but she also married Haynes after *she* proposed to *him*.

Haynes was ordained in 1785 and pastored for two years in Torrington, Connecticut. There he experienced some of the discrimination that would crop up throughout his life. One man in Torrington was so offended at the idea of a black pastor that he refused to attend church. When he finally did condescend to attend, the man refused to take off his hat but sat in the pew with it planted firmly on his head. Yet when Haynes started preaching, the scoffer was so impressed that he quietly took off his hat and put it under the seat and began to pay close attention.

SERVICE IN RUTLAND

In 1788 Lemuel Haynes and his family went to Rutland, Vermont, to take charge of the Congregational church there. Haynes ministered thirty years in Rutland. As odd as it may sound to modern ears, Vermont was part of the frontier at that time. Life was not as refined and civilized in the recesses of the Green Mountains as it was on the eastern seaboard.

Raised in a family touched by the Great Awakening, Lemuel Haynes ministered in Rutland during what is generally called the Second Great Awakening. This revival swept through the United States from the late 1790s until, perhaps, as late as the 1830s. In the "west" (areas such as Kentucky and Ohio), frontier camp meetings were the most visible expression of the revival. In the east, revivals tended to center in individual churches or in colleges. Yale, for example, experienced a series of revivals under the presidency of Timothy Dwight, a grandson of Jonathan Edwards.

Although he lived far from the large population centers on the East Coast, Lemuel Haynes saw the effects of the revival in Rutland. There were forty-six members in the church in Rutland when he came, and twenty-six more joined the first year. More dramatic awakenings were yet to come. In 1801 Haynes seemed to sense the approach of revival when he wrote to a friend, "When the enemy shall come in like a flood, the Spirit of the Lord shall lift up a standard against him. We have, of late, a little inquiry among some young people about religion. A number sent for me last Sabbath to converse about their souls's concern. Five or six children and youth are crying out, 'What shall we do to be saved?' I take a little courage that these few drops may presage a shower."

In 1803 Rutland experienced a remarkable revival. It began when a young person who had previously shown little interest in religion asked to meet with the pastor. Haynes decided to set up an inquiry meeting for all who were concerned about their souls. To his surprise, a large crowd showed up. Burdened with sin, people began holding prayer meetings in private houses. (In one such meeting, the crowd was so large that the floor collapsed and dumped the people into the cellar; however, no one was seriously hurt.) "Never did I behold such a winter as the past," Haynes wrote in April 1803. "We have been able to reap in the middle of January."

A total of 103 professed salvation and joined the church during the revival.

In 1808 another revival occurred, with 109 joining the church. In April of 1810 a joyful Haynes wrote, "It was truly a refreshing season. It astonished beholders. I could visit houses and see poor distressed creatures . . . crying out, 'What shall I do to be saved?' Blessed be God, we still see the effects of it." This revival was particularly dear to Haynes, as three of his own children were converted.

All was not revival triumph in Vermont, though. Like Bible-believing preachers of every age, Haynes found himself confronting the challenge of false religion. One of Vermont's own heroes, Revolutionary War commander Ethan Allen, was a crusader against Christianity. He wrote *Reason, the Only Oracle of Man,* a defense of deism, a religion that taught the idea of a "clockmaker God." According to the deists, God made the universe and set it in motion but then stepped back to have little to do with His creation. Deists denied the miraculous (such as Christ's supernatural character) and affirmed the absolute supremacy of reason. The support of leaders such as Allen made deism attractive to many would-be intellectuals in Vermont.

A more pressing problem to pastors such as Haynes was Universalism. As its name suggests, Universalism teaches that there is no hell, that all men will ultimately be saved. Furthermore, Universalists deny biblical teachings such as the deity of Jesus Christ and the necessity of His blood atonement for sin. The first major leader of Universalism in the United States was Hosea Ballou. A schoolteacher and preacher, Ballou traveled over New England, trying to win followers for his cause. In due course, he came to Rutland. Haynes attended the meeting and heard Ballou speak. Ballou had previously accused Haynes of cowardice for refusing to publicly dispute with him over Universalism. But on learning Haynes was present, the speaker asked him, as the local pastor, to offer some "remarks" at the close.

It may be that Haynes expected such an opportunity, for he got up and gave a full sermon: "Universal Salvation—A Very Ancient Doctrine." Haynes refuted the false doctrine not with blasts of invective but with deft satire. Universalism was indeed a very old teaching, Haynes admitted, as old as the Garden of Eden, where the serpent told Eve, "Ye shall not surely die." Haynes said, "I can see no injury done to the cause of God in giving the devil his due." Satan, said Haynes, was the first Universalist preacher, a preacher noted for his age, cunning, diligent labor, and success. "What Satan meant to preach," Haynes said, "was that there is no hell; and that the wages of sin is not death, but eternal life." The sermon hardly convinced Ballou, but the traveling Universalist must have felt the barb of Haynes's description of the Devil as "a certain preacher, in his journey, [who] came that way and disturbed their peace and tranquility by endeavoring to reverse the prohibition of the Almighty." Haynes successfully warned his people against the false teachings of Universalism by examining those teachings in the light of Scripture.

Shortly thereafter, Haynes published the sermon "Universal Salvation," and it became his most popular work, going through seventy editions between 1805 and 1860. It brought him fame outside the boundaries of Rutland. Universalists assailed him, often with racist jibes that his mind was as black as his skin. As the sermon demonstrated, however, Haynes was able to take care of himself in controversy. For example, it was probably the Universalist controversy that caused two young would-be wits to confront Haynes and ask, "Father Haynes, have you heard the good news?"

"No, what is it?" said Haynes.

"Why, the devil is dead," one replied.

Haynes looked at them sadly, placed his hands on their heads, and solemnly said, "Oh, poor fatherless children! what will become of you?"

As this story indicates, Lemuel Haynes was a man with a keen mind and quick wit. Acquaintances preserved many such tales about him. A doctor to whom Haynes owed money was moving away from Rutland. Haynes went to see the man, who was hardly known for his godly character, to pay the debt. Graciously, the doctor returned the money as a gift. Then he said, "But, Mr. Haynes, you must pray for me, and *make me a good man.*" Haynes looked at him and then replied, "Why, doctor, I think I had much better pay the debt."

Likewise Haynes once encountered a religious skeptic who asked the pastor on what evidence he believed the Bible. "Why, sir," Haynes said, "the Bible, which was written more than a thousand years ago, informs me that I should meet such a man as yourself." Scornfully, the man asked, "But how can you show that?" Haynes pointed him to II Peter 3:3—"There shall come in the last days scoffers, walking after their own lusts."

On another occasion, late in life, Haynes entered a hotel where several people were celebrating the election of Andrew Jackson as president, a man whom Haynes wholeheartedly opposed. They urged him to propose a toast to the new president. Haynes said simply, "Andrew Jackson, Psalm 109, verse 8," and left. After he was gone, they looked up the reference: "Let his days be few; and let another take his office."

Despite his long ministry in Rutland, Haynes's time there did not end happily. There was probably weariness on the part of some members of the congregation in having the same pastor for thirty years. The immediate cause of division was Haynes's political views. He was a member of the Federalist party, the party of Presidents George Washington and John Adams. Haynes loyally supported the Federalists and staunchly opposed the Republicans of Thomas Jefferson. Haynes opposed the War of 1812, for instance, as an unnecessary conflict caused by Republican bungling more than real grievances with the British. By 1818 such views were increasingly unpopular in Vermont. In the heat of this controversy, the race issue also came up. Haynes reported that it was as though after thirty years some of the people of Rutland suddenly discovered that their pastor was black. After meeting with his supporters and the church leaders, Haynes decided to leave without a fight.

Because the departure was peaceful, if strained, Haynes stayed on for a short time and preached a farewell sermon. He reminded the congregation that in his years in Rutland, he had preached over five thousand sermons, four hundred of them funeral sermons, and that the town had enjoyed two large revivals in that time. There was probably some bitterness at his treatment: "I am willing to repeat . . . in this public manner, that, had the people been united, wholesome discipline properly exercised, a firm and unshaken attachment to the cause of God manifested among all the professors of religion, I should have chosen to continue with you at the expense of temporal emolument; but, considering the divisions existing, and the uncommon stupidity prevalent, I have been fully satisfied that it was my duty to be dismissed, and have requested my friends not to oppose it." Yet he still had a pastor's love for his congregation: "My dear brethren and friends, I did not realize my attachment to you before the parting time came. Many disagreeable things have taken place; but still I feel my heart going out towards this people."

A MURDER MYSTERY

Haynes left Rutland and went to Manchester, Vermont, where he served as pastor from 1818 to 1822. Although it was a brief period in comparison to his stay at Rutland, it was made memorable by a murder mystery he confronted, a case worthy of Sherlock Holmes.

In 1813, before Haynes had come to Manchester, a mentally unbalanced man named Russell Colvin had disappeared. At first, his disappearance aroused little notice; he had vanished before and always shown up again later. When months passed and Colvin did not return, however, mutterings began to rumble about that he had been murdered. In the midst of this uneasy atmosphere, the uncle of Colvin's wife announced that three times he had had a dream in which Colvin appeared and said he had been murdered. Casting about in places where they thought a body *might* be buried, searchers dug in a pit used for burying potatoes and found a knife and a button that Colvin's wife said had belonged to her husband. In a hollow stump a dog found some bones and other remains that appeared to be human. The thought that Colvin had been murdered became a certainty to the townspeople of Manchester.

Suspicion fell on Colvin's brothers-in-law, Stephen and Jesse Boorn. The pair were questioned by the authorities but without result. Then as Jesse was on the verge of being released, he suddenly accused his brother of the crime. Apparently in a panic, he said that during an argument in a field Stephen had cracked Colvin on the back of the head with a tree limb and laid him out; Jesse could not explain what had happened to the body. Now Colvin's son announced that he had seen Stephen Boorn strike Colvin, but the boy had run away and not spoken out of fear. Stephen and Jesse Boorn were brought to trial and were convicted on October 31, 1819. The court sentenced them to be hanged on January 28, 1820.

It was during the arrest and trial of the Boorns that Lemuel Haynes became involved in the case. As the local pastor, he visited them in prison, trying to win them to Christ, and he became convinced they were innocent. On one occasion, Stephen said to Haynes, "I am as innocent as Jesus Christ!" Haynes instantly rebuked him for this outrageous statement. Chastened, Stephen replied, "I don't mean that I am guiltless as he was; I know I am a great sinner; but I am as innocent of killing Colvin as he was." The Boorns appealed to the state legislature. Jesse's sentence was commuted to life imprisonment but Stephen's was not. In prison, facing death, Stephen began to read the Scriptures. He told the pastor, "Mr. Haynes, I see no way but I must die; every thing works against me; but I am an innocent man; this you will know after I am dead." He asked Haynes to pray and stood bound in chains in his cell as the pastor prayed with him.

Just a little over a month before Stephen Boorn was to hang, a cry rang through the streets of Manchester—"Colvin has come!" A man in New Jersey read the account of the Boorn trial and was astonished. He knew that Russell Colvin was alive and living in New Jersey. Quickly, Colvin was brought back to Manchester. Colvin was still mentally unbalanced, but he was very much alive. Stephen Boorn was brought out of prison so quickly at the news that his leg manacles were still on. When the convicted murderer and his supposed victim met, Colvin looked at the chains and asked, "What is that for?" Boorn said, "Because they say I murdered you." Colvin replied, "You never hurt me."

The return of Colvin and the release of the Boorns was a cause for general rejoicing. Haynes published an account of the Colvin mystery that was widely read in its day. Also Haynes preached a sermon "The Prisoner Released," using the Boorn-Colvin case as an illustration of how a man may be released from sin's imprisonment. Stephen Boorn himself experienced both kinds of deliverance. Through the witness of Haynes during that terrible time, Boorn was converted to Christ.

FINAL YEARS

In 1822 Haynes moved to Granville, New York, where he spent the last eleven years of his life. He served as pastor of the Congregational church there and in 1831 saw another revival of religion under his ministry, one in which fifty people were converted.

In 1833 Haynes made a final visit to Granville, Massachusetts, the place where he had grown up in the Rose household, where he had found Christ, and where he had entered the ministry. Although he was invited there to preach, Haynes gladly took the opportunity to revisit the scenes of his childhood. Accompanied by a younger man, he visited the old Rose home, pointing to the chimney he had helped build as a young man. He saw the fields where he had worked and visited the cemetery where he noted the graves of people who had professed Christ under his ministry. Finally, he visited the old apple tree—still standing—where he had found Christ.

The trip was almost the last major event of his life as Haynes's health began to decline rapidly. On his deathbed, he said, "I have been examining myself and looking back upon my past life, but I can find nothing in myself and nothing in all my past services to recommend me at the bar of Jehovah. Christ is my all. His blood is my only hope of acceptance." He died September 28, 1833. His epitaph read as follows: "Here lies the dust of a poor hell-deserving sinner, who ventured into eternity trusting wholly on the merits of Christ for salvation. In the full belief of the great doctrines he preached while on earth, he invites his children, and all who read this, to trust their eternal interest on the same foundation."

For Further Reading

Bogin, Ruth. " 'Liberty Further Extended': A 1776 Antislavery Manuscript by Lemuel Haynes." *William and Mary Quarterly* 40 (1983): 85-105.

Cooley, Timothy Mather. *Sketches of the Life and Character of the Rev. Lemuel Haynes.* 1837. Reprint. New York: Negro Universities Press, 1969.

Haynes, Lemuel. *Black Preacher to White America: The Collected Writings of Lemuel Haynes, 1774-1833.* Edited by Richard Newman. Brooklyn: Carlson, 1990.

"Lemuel Haynes." In *Annals of the American Pulpit,* edited by William B. Sprague. Vol. 2, Part 2. Trinitarian Congregational. Reprint. New York: Arno Press, 1969, pp. 176-87.

Newman, Richard. *Lemuel Haynes: A Bio-Bibliography.* New York: Lambeth Press, 1984.

Today, most Americans are keenly aware of the injustice of slavery as it existed in the United States before the Civil War. Many are not aware, however, of the difficulties also faced by free blacks in America at that time. In both North and South, the majority of free blacks did not enjoy the full range of rights and privileges whites enjoyed. They often could not vote, and some states actually wrote clauses into their constitutions prohibiting free blacks from entering their borders. Slavery, it seems, was but one expression of the larger sin of racism.

Many blacks fought courageously against discrimination. African American Christians knew their dignity before God and refused to surrender their self-respect. They also refused to let discrimination keep them from ministering to the spiritual needs of their fellow man. A case in point is John Chavis, black minister and educator. His sometimes painful, even humiliating story illustrates the struggles and pressures that free blacks faced in the pre–Civil War South. Yet his life also demonstrates the strength of a man who refused to be relegated to the status of a second-class citizen.

MYSTERY YEARS

Tracing the events of John Chavis's early life is like being a detective putting together scattered clues to solve a mystery. It is only from brief, fragmented records that we know anything of the first forty years of his life. All we know from John Chavis himself about these early years is a brief reference in a letter in which he describes himself as a "free-born American and a revolutionary soldier." He was born around 1763, but the place is unknown. One tale says that he was born in the West Indies and came to America at an early age. More likely is the account that he was born in North Carolina or perhaps Virginia, a view supported by Chavis's own reference to himself as a "free-born American." There is a record of a "John Chavis" living as an indentured servant in North Carolina in 1773 who could have been the same man. Military records show that during the American Revolution Chavis enlisted in the Fifth Virginia Regiment in 1778 and served three years. His captain reported that Chavis had "faithfully fulfilled [his duties] and is thereby entitled to all immunities granted to three year soldiers." He is also noted in Virginia tax records for 1789, records that show his total taxable property as a single horse.

Chavis was working as a tutor at the time of that tax record, demonstrating that he must have been able to get some education as a young man. There is also evidence (scanty as the rest) that after that time Chavis attended Princeton College. The minutes of the trustees of Princeton for 1792 contain a recommendation that "John Chavis," described as "a free black" from Virginia, be "received" under a fund established for the education of financially needy students preparing for the Presbyterian ministry. His name is also found on a list of students who attended the college but did not graduate. Several stories about Chavis's experiences at Princeton circulated long after his death. One tale implied that he was sent to Princeton on a bet over whether a black man could be educated. If so, whoever bet on Chavis won handily. An even more common story states that Chavis was a private student of John Witherspoon (died 1794), the president of Princeton and the only clergyman to sign the Declaration of Independence. This account is at least possible. Witherspoon is known to have served as a tutor on a special basis to a few black and Indian students. It is almost certain that Chavis attended Washington Academy (now Washington and Lee University) in Lexington, Virginia, sometime before 1802. Although the details of John Chavis's education may be hazy, he unquestionably received schooling superior to that of most American blacks of his time.

REVIVAL PREACHER

After completing his education, Chavis entered the Presbyterian ministry. It was a dramatic period in America's religious history, the midst of the Second Great Awakening, sometimes called the Great Revival in the South and West. The Holy Spirit was sweeping across the American landscape, drawing multitudes to Christ. The revival did not occur among large masses of city dwellers gathered in huge city-wide campaigns. Instead, many faithful preachers traveled from town to town and settlement to settlement preaching to small groups ranging in size from a few hundred to a few dozen. John Chavis was one of those preachers. His local presbytery licensed him to preach in November 1800. Denominational records describe him as "of unquestionably good fame" and express the hope that "as he is a man of colour he may be peculiarly useful to those of his own complexion" in preaching the gospel. He preached his trial sermon in 1801 on the text "Believe on the Lord Jesus Christ, and thou shalt be saved" (Acts 16:31).

From 1801 to 1807 Chavis served as a missionary/evangelist in Maryland, Virginia, and North Carolina. Details of his preaching tours are disappointingly slim. The description of Chavis's first tours of Virginia and North Carolina by the Presbyterian missions committee gives little more than scattered comments along with dry records of the number of sermons preached, the number of persons attending, and the amount of money collected. In Virginia he preached 23 times to a total of 2,610 people. In Lexington, Virginia, he reported "a revival of religion" and in another place "a revival of religion among the Baptists." (Although a Presbyterian, he also preached in Baptist and Methodist churches when they invited him.) In Coal River, the record states, "Here one opposer of religion was made to fall and weep. He never saw a people more desirous to be instructed." In Greenbriar County, a "number appeared to be deeply imprest; he was strongly solicited to settle here," that is, settle as a minister. The North Carolina tour was even more extensive, involving 68 sermons to a total of 7,005 hearers.

One characteristic of these tours surprised the Presbyterian committee—no more than a fourth of Chavis's hearers were black. The committee in fact complained that he was speaking to more whites than blacks, which was not the idea when they sent him out. (Years later a rather snide obituary in a Presbyterian newspaper said bluntly, "Although he was not as useful, as it had been hoped he would be [in reaching blacks], yet his Christian character gave comfort to his friends.") The problem, Chavis had discovered, was that the poorly educated slaves often preferred more emotionalism in their sermons than he was prepared to give them. After hearing Chavis's explanation, the church modified his commission, telling him to work "among the blacks and free people of colour . . . , if practicable, otherwise at his discretion."

Unfortunately, we have none of his sermons preserved. In fact, only a few passing references survive to describe his work as a preacher. In January 1802, for instance, Ann Smith of Granville County, North Carolina, briefly noted in a letter "The Great Revival of Religion" in Hawfields, speaking of how "this great work was going forward" under the ministry of Chavis and others. A lawyer in Granville County recalled something of Chavis's style: "I have heard him read and explain the Scriptures to my father's family repeatedly. His English was remarkably pure . . . his manner was impressive, his explanations clear and concise, and his views . . . entirely orthodox." Chavis moved from Virginia to North Carolina during the latter part of his preaching tours. After he settled in North Carolina, he gave up his traveling ministry. He continued to preach, however (although he never pastored a church), until the 1830s when a backlash against black preaching (discussed later) shut pulpits to him.

EDUCATOR

With his move to North Carolina, John Chavis went from being primarily a preacher to being primarily a teacher. He first tried to integrate white and free black students in his school, but he ran into opposition from white parents. Therefore, he began teaching black students in the evening and reserving the daytime instruction for whites. An 1808 notice in a Raleigh newspaper told parents of prospective students, "Those who think proper to put their children under his care, may rely upon the strictest attention being paid not only to their Education, but to their morals, which he deems an *important* part of Education."

Teaching was a sometimes uncertain way to make a living. He was a private tutor depending on student tuition for his support, not a salaried teacher in a state-run school. Often, he had to supplement his income by farming. Although all who observed Chavis's work approved of the quality, he had to struggle at times to acquire students. In 1825 he wrote, "I am placed in the most unhappy situation. I am in want of everything and without a school and what to do I know not. I hope however that God has in reserve some way of relief. It is commonly said that the darkest time is just before day." Later that year he noted that he was trying to start a school in Hillsborough. Failing that, a local planter thought he could help Chavis get twenty-five students at "$10 each" in Ellibies Creek, just north of Durham, but by 1828 his school had only sixteen pupils, and it was hard to make ends meet.

John Chavis taught the children of several prominent North Carolina families, including the children of senators, governors, and judges. These students remembered him fondly and years later praised his talents as a teacher. But he also maintained his evening school for free blacks. In 1830 the editor of the *Raleigh Review* attended one of these evening sessions. Reporting the incident in his paper, the editor used a condescending tone, but it is evident that John Chavis touched the lives of his black students.

> On Friday last, we attended an examination of the free children of color, attached to the school conducted by *John Chavis,* also colored, but a regularly educated Presbyterian

minister, and we have seldom received more gratification from any exhibition of a similar character. To witness a well regulated school, composed of this class of persons—to see them setting an example both in behavior and scholarship, which their *white* superiors might take pride in imitating, was a cheering spectacle to a philanthropist. The exercises throughout, evinced a degree of attention and assiduous care on the part of the instructor, highly creditable, and of attainment on the part of his scholars almost incredible. We were also much pleased with the sensible address which closed the examination. The object of the respectable teacher, was to impress on the scholars, the fact, that they occupied an inferior and subordinate station in society, and were possessed but of limited privileges; but that even *they* might become useful in their particular sphere by making a proper improvement of the advantages afforded them.

Obviously, Chavis gave his black students instruction of a quality that most whites of that time found unsurpassed. In doing so, he gave them a great gift and, perhaps, hope—something that most blacks in the South at that time did not have.

SOCIAL AND POLITICAL VIEWS

John Chavis's social and political views are preserved for us in part in his many letters to Willie P. Mangum, a United States senator from North Carolina. The correspondence between these two demonstrates an unusual familiarity between a free black preacher and teacher and a prominent white Southern politician. Some members of Mangum's family were taught by Chavis, and there are stories (never substantiated) that Chavis taught Mangum himself. Just how exceptional their relationship was is illustrated by the recollections of the husband of Mangum's granddaughter. He recalled how Chavis was treated as an equal in Mangum's home, much to the amazement of the children of the household who were not used to seeing blacks received so. They were quickly quieted with the warning "Hush, child, he is your father's friend."

Chavis offered Senator Mangum advice on a wide variety of subjects. For example, he opposed the idea of amending the Constitution "because once a beginning is made to amend the constitution, away goes the best of human compacts. . . . The truth is, the Constitution as it now stands places the people upon firm ground, that they cannot sink or stop."

Chavis was a staunch Federalist, a follower of the party of George Washington and Alexander Hamilton that favored a strong central government. Chavis complained when Mangum once said "in broad open daylight" that the black preacher "had become unsound in politics." Chavis replied, "No Sir, I would have to know, that I am the same genuine, undeviating, unshaken lump of Federalism that I ever was, that I have never deviated a single hair's breadth, from Dan to Beersheba . . . because I believe that Federal policy to be the best that ever was adopted in this or in other Country, of a free and elective government. That there is no other policy that can stand the shock and vicissitudes of human nature." Understanding the Bible's teaching concerning human sinfulness, Chavis believed that only the Federalists favored the strong government policies "sufficient to restrain the corruptions of human nature."

Chavis's politics colored his views of the political leaders of the day. He admired Henry Clay, "an honest, intelligent, and tried patriot and of inflexible integrity." He staunchly opposed Andrew Jackson: "I believe him to be an honest man, but there is no other trait in his character, in my estimation, that qualifies him for the seat of a Chief Magistrate." He spoke of Jackson's "domineering and despotic disposition" and said "that the United States would be too poor to induce me to vote for the reelection of G[eneral] J[ackson]."

What is most surprising to the modern reader are Chavis's views on slavery. In 1805, during his preaching tours, Chavis encountered a black woman who "expressed her gratitude that God had brought her from her native country to this land of Gospel light and liberty" and said that "all the blacks ought to be thankful that they were in a country where they could hear the name of the blessed Jesus, and know how to escape from the bondage of the devil." Chavis approved of her sentiments and noted, "I joined with this my sister in saying that it is truly a matter of thankfulness to the black people, that they were brought to this country for I believe thousands of them will have reason to rejoice for it in the ages of eternity."

Even more astonishing is Chavis's opposition to the abolition of slavery. "I believe that there are a part of the abolitionists that have, and do, act . . . from pure motives," he said, "but I think they have zeal without knowledge, and are doing more mischief than they expect." In 1836 he wrote to Mangum to urge him to oppose the idea of abolishing slavery in the District of Columbia. Chavis considered slaves to be simply property, "the property of the holder equal to his cow or his horse," and maintained that the government had no right to seize anyone's property. He said,

That slavery is a national evil no one doubts, but what is to be done? It exists and what can be done with [it]? All that can be done, is to make the best of a bad bargain. For I am clearly of the opinion that immediate emancipation would be to entail the greatest earthly curse upon my brethren according to the flesh that could be conferred upon them especially in a country like ours. I suppose if they knew I said this they would be ready to take my life, but as I wish them well, I feel no disposition to see them any more miserable than they are.

Chavis's views on slavery represented the position of only a small minority among American blacks, but such views were not unknown. Apparently some free blacks living in the South before the Civil War sincerely thought the immediate (as opposed to a gradual) abolition of slavery would be harmful to blacks. Daniel Payne, later a bishop in the African Methodist Episcopal Church, admitted that when he lived as a free black in Charleston, South Carolina, he believed in gradual emancipation so that blacks could be educated first. It was after he moved to the North, Payne said, that he was convinced that blacks could never be properly educated while bound in slavery. John Chavis at least strove to educate blacks and seemed to feel compassion for the "miserable" status of the slaves. Furthermore, as one of his biographers notes in his defense, Chavis was apparently the first educator to attempt, however briefly, a racially integrated school in North Carolina. Chavis was no progressive pioneer against slavery, but neither was he completely insensitive to the plight of his fellow African Americans.

FINAL YEARS

John Chavis's final years were hard ones. His wife, Frances, was an invalid, and Chavis said in a letter in 1833 that he had little hope of her ever getting better. Ironically, she survived him by a few years. Events in Virginia over which Chavis had no control would affect him even more. In 1831 a slave preacher named Nat Turner in Southampton County, Virginia, led a slave rebellion. In the initial violence of the uprising and the brutal retaliation that followed, about sixty whites and a hundred blacks died. The revolt frightened the slave-holding South, and Southern legislatures began passing a series of laws to make sure such uprisings did not occur again.

Chavis called Turner's revolt "that abominable insurrection in Southampton," but he was not spared in the backlash. A new North Carolina law decreed that no black—free or slave—could preach in public or address any private worship service where the slaves of more than one family were gathered. The penalty for violating the law was thirty-nine lashes. Chavis found that pulpits which had been open to him for years were now closed. Chavis had also delighted in his heavy involvement in politics as he sought to influence his community, state, and nation for what he saw as right. That involvement also came to an abrupt end when North Carolina took the right to vote from free blacks in 1835.

Chavis could still teach, but he found even that occupation more difficult to pursue. Teaching had never been extremely profitable in Chavis's best days. By the 1830s it was even harder to get enough paying students to make a living, and some whites began to criticize his efforts to teach free blacks. On top of this, the aging teacher was experiencing physical problems. He lamented to Mangum in 1833 that he would "not be able to teach long for I am losing my hearing fast. Then what shall I do?"

Life became very difficult for John Chavis as age, infirmity, and finally poverty took their toll. A Presbyterian pastor noted to a friend in 1834 that he had received a letter from Chavis in which the teacher called himself "a miserable man—Old and infirm—his wife a dying—or at least on her death-bed—in want of the necessaries of life—and without money to procure them." Chavis wrote to Mangum in 1837 that he expected to visit Mrs. Mangum "if I can get any clothes fit to wear for I am naked at this time, and how I am to be clothed I don't know." A former student recalled having visited Chavis and "found his old teacher in great poverty, living with some free-negroes—a complete wreck of his former self." Chavis himself told Mangum in 1836, "I am done, the pressure of this winter has put it out of my power to keep house after this year—but must depend solely and alone upon the bounty of my friends, a painful consideration."

John Chavis was not completely forgotten, however. An 1880 account recalled a happy reunion for Chavis: "The writer remembers to have seen him when a short time before his death several of his white pupils, prominent gentlemen, called to see him. Chavis was then advanced in years, his white hair forming a strange contrast to his ebony face for he was of unmixed African descent. His manners were dignified yet respectful and entirely unassuming and his conversation sprightly and interesting." The Presbyterian church also offered some relief. Although it advised him not to fight the law against black preaching, the church gave him a pension of $50 a year until his death "for the support of this aged laborer in the Lord's vineyard" and after his death for the support of

his invalid wife. When informed of his pension, Chavis said grate-
fully, "I view this Presbyterial arrangement as a merciful providence for which I am thankful." He died on June 15, 1838.

HERITAGE

The son of an acquaintance of John Chavis wrote in 1889,
"Chavis was a wonderful man, fully equipped for the work he was
doing both as teacher and preacher, and has merited a higher place
in our esteem than has been accorded him." Admittedly, Chavis is
not as fondly remembered as some other black heroes. His views
on slavery and the scattered, fragmented sources on his life make
it difficult to appreciate him. Yet in his letters to Willie Mangum,
one sees in John Chavis's character an unbending dignity. He attempted always to excel and to transcend the obstacles he faced.
His talents as a speaker and educator were so unquestionably apparent that virtually all who knew him acknowledged them—even
though some fell back on the flimsy argument that he was somehow different from other blacks.

In 1938, on the one hundredth anniversary of his death, North
Carolina named a park after Chavis in Raleigh and erected a historical marker saying—

JOHN CHAVIS

Early 19th Century Free Negro preacher and teacher
of both races in North Carolina.

The marker capsulizes his career better perhaps than its sponsors
intended. John Chavis was a minister to "both races." Whether
ministering as a preacher in the Second Great Awakening or as a
schoolteacher in North Carolina, Chavis used his gifts to reach out
to both blacks and whites. His life was a testimony to the equality
of the races, of what a black man or woman could be if not enslaved and if given a chance to prove himself or herself. Giving to
others and providing an example to others—that is no small heritage. And it is the heritage of John Chavis.

For Further Reading

Brawley, Benjamin. *Negro Builders and Heroes*. Chapel Hill: University of North Carolina Press, 1937.

Franklin, John Hope. *The Free Negro in North Carolina 1790-1860*.
1943. Reprint. New York: Russell and Russell, 1969.

Knight, E. W. "Notes on John Chavis." *North Carolina Historical Review* 7 (1930): 326-45.

Two sad blots on America's history have been the nation's treatment of the Indians and its enslavement of African Americans. In one case, greedy men deprived the Native Americans of their land and livelihood; in the other, they deprived Africans of their liberty. Yet some white men and women looked with compassion on these peoples whom other whites despised, and they proclaimed to them the message of salvation through Christ. The preaching of the gospel to Indians and blacks did not erase the injustice done to these peoples, nor did it release their oppressors from the guilt of their actions. But the gospel became the "pearl of great price"— the most precious possession—of many blacks and Indians who gladly heard the message of deliverance from bondage to sin. One African American both heard the truth gladly and then earnestly declared it to Native Americans. He was John Stewart, missionary to the Indians.

INDIAN MISSIONS IN NORTH AMERICA

When John Stewart began his mission work, he embarked on a work that had a heritage almost as old as the founding of the colonies. In Puritan New England, for example, John Eliot (1604-90) labored among the Algonquins. He learned their language and translated the Bible into Algonquin. About four thousand "praying Indians" (as they were known) became Christians. A little farther south, the Moravians established works such as Gnadenhütten ("sheltered by grace") among the tribes in Pennsylvania. Yet both of these efforts came to tragic ends. The Christian Algonquins were virtually wiped out when caught in the middle of a war between their fellow Indians and the English settlers. The Indians did not trust them because they were Christians, and the English did not trust them because they were Indians. The Moravian Indians likewise suffered the ravages of both whites and non-Christian Indians. In one of the worst atrocities, American troops massacred some ninety Moravian Indians near the end of the American Revolution.

With such a history, it is not surprising that many Indians viewed the coming of white missionaries with suspicion. In 1805 a

63

missionary met with the leaders of the Iroquois League in New York State to ask whether he might be allowed to preach the gospel among them. Seneca chief Sagu-yu-what-hah, better known to whites as Red Jacket, replied to him on behalf of the Iroquois.

The chief reviewed the history of relations between whites and Indians. He pointed out how the first white settlers "had fled from their own country for fear of wicked men, and had come here to enjoy their religion." Yet, Red Jacket noted, the whites had made war on the Indians, had come in ever greater numbers, and had taken Indian lands. Above all, he asked the missionary why the Iroquois should abandon their old religion and accept that of the white man when it seemed to make the whites no better than the Indians. Red Jacket said, "We are told that you have been preaching to the white people in this place. These people are our neighbors. We are acquainted with them. We will wait a little while, and see what effect your preaching has upon them. If we find it does them good, makes them honest and less disposed to cheat Indians, we will then consider again of what you have said."

Early Years and Conversion

John Stewart was born around 1786 not as a slave but as a free man in Powhatan County, Virginia. His parents were devoutly religious and his brother became a Baptist preacher, but Stewart's "faith" was only on the surface, not in his heart. When he was twenty-one, his parents moved to Tennessee. Ill at the time they left, John followed later but on the way was robbed of everything that he owned. In despair and discouragement, he stopped in Marietta, Ohio. There he descended into alcoholism, hoping either to drown his sorrows or to kill himself outright.

Perhaps some of his parents' influence remained, for in his depths he tried to reform himself. Stewart got a job making sugar and spent his spare time praying and reading the Bible. The efforts at reform did not last, though. He bounced between despair and drunken carousing. One day Stewart would long for deliverance from his sense of sinfulness. The next he would go off on another binge. Sometimes Stewart walked along the Ohio River, thinking of throwing himself in and ending—he thought—his misery.

Finally, Stewart went into business as a dyer and again devoted all his spare moments to prayer. When he reached the lowest depths of hopelessness, he found deliverance. Like a drowning man clutching at anything that might keep him afloat, Stewart threw himself on Christ and cried, "Lord, save or I perish!" The Holy

Spirit made the change in Stewart's life that he could never have effected by his own efforts at reform.

Stewart was a new creature in Christ, but his early growth as a believer was fitful. Reared a Baptist, young Stewart thought that he should align with that group. But since there was no Baptist congregation in the area, he did not join a church. Soon he began to backslide and doubt his salvation, and he began sinking into misery again. Then during an evening walk he heard the singing from a Methodist prayer meeting. Stewart joined them and found comfort in their fellowship. Later he attended a camp meeting, and after a night of earnest, searching prayer, he found peace and assurance.

MISSIONARY TO THE INDIANS

After this renewed commitment to Christ, Stewart then felt impelled to proclaim the gospel to others. He said that it seemed as though he heard a voice that said, "Thou shalt declare my counsel faithfully." Like Jonah refusing to go to Nineveh, John resisted and even planned to go south to Tennessee because he felt that God wanted him to go north to preach. An illness, instead of a great fish, stopped him. When he recovered, Stewart gave in and headed north into Indian country.

Much of northern Ohio was still wilderness in the early 1800s. It had been the site of bloody fighting between whites and Indians during General "Mad" Anthony Wayne's Fallen Timbers campaign in the 1790s and again during the War of 1812. Peace had come to the region only shortly before Stewart arrived there. He preached first to a group of Delawares on the Sandusky River. Stewart, who had a fine singing voice, sang hymns, which entertained them, and spoke through an interpreter. The Delawares listened politely, with some interest. Still restless, Stewart pushed farther northwest to the Wyandot reservation at Upper Sandusky, Ohio, in November 1816. It was there he would have his greatest ministry.

The Wyandots to whom he came were a branch of the Hurons, a tribe that originally had lived in what is now southern Ontario, Canada. With the coming of the white Europeans, the Hurons had built a profitable fur trade with the French. In doing so, however, they drew the attention of the powerful Iroquois League. Viewing the Hurons as a threat, the Iroquois waged a war of extermination against them from 1649 to 1651. The tribe was scattered, with pockets of survivors finding refuge in places such as Quebec and Detroit. One branch, the Wyandots, settled in what is now Ohio.

By sale and treaty, the government finally reduced Wyandot territory to a small reservation on the upper reaches of the Sandusky River in northern Ohio. In a letter Stewart described their simple manner of life when he first arrived: "Some of their houses were made of small poles, and covered with bark, others of bark altogether. Their farms contained from about two acres to less than half an acre. The women did nearly all the work that was done. They had as many as two plows in the nation; but these were seldom used." It was to this people that Stewart came and ministered.

Stewart met the Indian agent, William Walker, the white government representative responsible for the care of the reservation. Walker in turn introduced Stewart to Jonathan Pointer, another black, who knew the Wyandot language. Pointer had little interest in religion and was unenthusiastic about Stewart's plans. He told the would-be missionary bluntly that it was "folly" for him to preach to the Indians. Well-educated white men had preached without effect to the Indians, Pointer said, so how could Stewart, a poor black man, hope to succeed? Even when he agreed to interpret, Pointer would interject comments in his translation such as "so he says, I do not know whether it is so or not, nor do I care; all I care about is to interpret faithfully what he says, to you; you must not think that I care whether you believe it or not."

Stewart's reception was mixed. The Indians were friendly and polite, but they did not rush to embrace his religion. Many Wyandots still followed the traditional Indian religions, and some had been exposed to Roman Catholicism. Those familiar with Catholicism declared that Stewart's Bible was a false book, not like the one used by the Catholic priests. In addition, some white traders, who resented Stewart's work, told the Indians that Stewart was a runaway slave who had come to the reservation only to hide and escape capture.

Indian agent Walker was a great help in this situation. He called an assembly and solemnly proclaimed that Stewart's Bible was indeed the Word of God. He explained the differences to the doubters by noting that Stewart's Bible was in English and the Catholic one was in Latin. Some Indians, influenced by the lies of the white traders, had questioned Stewart's position as a preacher. Walker replied to them that there was no problem in what Stewart was doing as long as he did not conduct marriages or baptize anyone, because "any man has a right to talk about religion, and try to get others to embrace it."

The Wyandots generally listened to Stewart and many expressed an interest in following Christianity, but there were still no public conversions. Only a handful seemed to embrace Christ, and then only hesitantly. Then on a Wednesday in February 1817 (about three months after he had started working with the tribe), Stewart preached on the final judgment. There was pronounced restlessness among the congregation. The missionary held a prayer meeting later that day and exhorted the Indians to repent and trust in Christ. Suddenly, some began to fall to the ground and cry out for mercy. One sixty-year-old woman rose up from prayer and declared "that God, for Jesus's sake, had forgiven all her sins," and she began to urge the truth of Stewart's words to the crowds. Some of the Wyandots watching these actions became afraid and said that the convicted were dying or crazy. Stewart said, "They are not dying; neither are they insane, as you suppose; though some of them, I trust, are dying to sin and struggling into a life of righteousness, peace and joy in the Holy Ghost." But despite all the public mourning, only the woman who testified professed conversion to Christ that night.

A few days later, Stewart observed a Wyandot religious dance. The following Sunday he said, "I have faithfully warned you that your feasts, dances, sacrifices . . . will never save you from your sins, and if you are never saved from your sins, where God is, you never can come." At that point, says Stewart's biographer, only about twenty out of the seven hundred or so Wyandots could be said to have shown any sign at all of having trusted in Christ. Stewart then left them to return to Marietta, for he still considered his mission work a short-term ministry. He promised, however, to try to return by June.

RETURN TO THE WYANDOTS

On May 25, 1817, Stewart sent a letter for William Walker to read to the Indians. He explained that he could not be back by June because of a leg injury he had suffered. In the meantime, he sent a sermon to be read to the Wyandots. Stewart urged Walker to inform them "that their hearts should be constantly set upon the Supreme Being who created them; and that it is their duty to raise their voices in praising, adoring, and loving that *Jesus,* who has suffered and died for them."

The sermon he sent was based on the text "Blessed are they which do hunger and thirst after righteousness: for they shall be filled" (Matt. 5:6). "These words were spoken by our Saviour Jesus

Christ," Stewart wrote, "and they are firm and sure; for his words are more firm than the heavens or the earth." He described for them the freedom that Christ offers: "This blessed Saviour shews his face with ten thousand smiles—lays his hand to the work—breaks the snares of sin—unlooses him from the fetters and chains of unbelief—sets the soul at liberty—puts a new song in his mouth—makes the soul rejoice with joy unspeakable and full of glory." This was by no means a "white man's religion" as Stewart presented it: "My friends, be glad and rejoice in the Lord, for this promise is to you and to all mankind." He closed with stern warnings of damnation awaiting those who would not repent but urged, "Now, my friends, you who have been at war against this great friend of sinners, now turn, for behold now is the accepted time, now is the day of salvation."

Stewart was able to return to the reservation in July 1817 and began preaching again. He faced fresh opposition, particularly from two chiefs who defended the traditional Indian religions. One chief, named Two Logs, opposed him publicly, even saying that Stewart, as a black man, was not worthy to preach to Indians. "The Great Spirit never created Negroes," Two Logs said; "they were created by the Evil Spirit." A woman claimed to have had a vision in which the God of the Indians told her not to listen to Stewart. The preacher in turn confronted her and said that there was not a "God of the Indians" but only one God, the one who had made all races. Others spread a rumor of a supposed old prophecy. They claimed that it had been prophesied that the white man would come to their land and reduce the Indians to tiny holdings (as had happened). Then a black man would come pretending friendship only to complete the destruction of the Indians. One staunch opponent of the missionary and defender of the traditional Indian religion said, "Well, the white man's religion may go on from house to house, until the whole nation embraces it, but when it comes to my house, it must there stop."

Surprisingly, some of the opposition that Stewart faced came from quarters where he would have expected his greatest support. After his return, some other missionaries came to the area and preached to the Wyandots. Impressed by Stewart's work, they offered to make him a regular salaried missionary of their organization. (Sources do not record what their organization was.) Because of some doctrinal difference, he refused their offer. Angered, the other missionaries began complaining that he was not a regular minister and had no authority to do the work he was doing. His Indian opponents seized on this criticism to discredit Stewart's work.

Therefore, Stewart and some of the Wyandots converted under his ministry traveled over fifty miles to present this problem to Methodist officials. This was the first the astonished officials had even heard of Stewart's work. Listening to the testimony of Stewart and his converts, the Methodists gladly licensed Stewart as a preacher of the gospel.

John Stewart saw a gradual growth—hesitant professions by a few, marked by backslidings, growing slowly to firmer conviction and larger numbers. He continued preaching but saw the most dramatic results when he entered the houses of the Wyandots and spoke personally with individuals. The converts often did not find being a Christian an easy road to travel. For instance, Catharine Warpole, the wife of a chief, listened to Stewart's preaching and was converted. Her husband, returning from a hunting trip to learn this, was furious. He first tried persuasion and then turned to beating her to force her to give up her new faith. Finally he abandoned her and went to live with another woman.

The Wyandots increasingly came to accept the black preacher. When the Treaty of Fort Meigs (1817) between the Wyandots and the U.S. government provided for a missionary to be settled among the tribe, they requested that the missionary be Stewart. The work also became a little easier as some of the chiefs of the tribe accepted Christianity. The first chief to convert was Matthew Peacock in late 1819. Other chiefs soon followed. One converted chief offered this testimony:

> A black man, Stewart, our brother here, came to us, and told us he was sent by the Great Spirit to tell us the true and good way. But we thought he was like all the rest—that he too wanted to cheat us, and get our money and land from us. He told us of all our sins; showed that drinking whisky was ruining us; that the Great Spirit was angry with us; and that we must leave off these things. But we treated him ill, and gave him little to eat, and trampled on him, and were jealous of him for a whole year. We are sure, if the Great Spirit had not sent him, he could not have borne with our treatment. . . .
>
> So we attended his meeting in the council-house, and the Great Spirit came upon us so that some cried aloud, some clapped their hands, some ran away, and some were angry. We held our meeting all night, sometimes singing and sometimes praying. By this time we were convinced that God had sent him to us.

Even Two Logs—the chief who had defended traditional Indian ways and declared it an insult for a black man to preach to Indians—was finally converted. Two Logs had been fierce in his opposition to Christianity, and he had threatened his own brother when he became a Christian. But an illness brought Two Logs low, and he could find no comfort in his old religion. Two Logs turned to Christ and found peace.

John Stewart's last years were marked by growing success. He was married in 1818 and his new wife, Polly, accompanied him back to the work. Other missionaries came to help Stewart and were accepted by the Indians, mainly because they were friends of Stewart. Building on Stewart's work, one missionary was able to construct both a school and a church building. Stewart himself was hampered by health problems, apparently tuberculosis resulting from his early bouts with alcoholism. Being unable at times to travel or even to preach, he set up a small school of a dozen or so Indian children whom he taught in his home. He fell seriously ill in the fall of 1823, declined rapidly, and finally died on December 17. His last words were "Be faithful."

After Stewart's death, the federal government pursued its policy of "Indian removal," the moving of tribes to reservations west of the Mississippi River. The government moved the Wyandots westward from their home on the Upper Sandusky to Kansas in 1843. Stewart's influence lived on, however, in the lives of tribe members whom he had touched.

John Stewart is today considered a founder of Methodist missions in America. He launched what may have been the first Methodist mission in North America, and he unquestionably helped inspire the formation of the Methodist Missionary Society. The Wyandot Mission in Upper Sandusky, Ohio, is now a Methodist shrine, and John Stewart lies buried on the grounds. As a man of color preaching to men of another color, John Stewart was a shining example of "the new man, which is renewed in knowledge after the image of him that created him: where there is neither Greek nor Jew, circumcision nor uncircumcision, Barbarian, Scythian, bond nor free: but Christ is all, and in all" (Col. 3:10-11).

For Further Reading

Marsh, Thelma R. *Moccasin Trails to the Cross: A History of the Mission to the Wyandott Indians on the Sandusky Plains.* Upper Sandusky, Ohio: United Methodist Historical Society of Ohio, 1974.

Mitchell, Joseph. *The Missionary Pioneer; or a Brief Memoir of the Life, Labours, and Death of John Stewart, Man of Color.* 1827. Reprint. Austin: The Pemberton Press, 1969.

Englishman William Carey, who went as a missionary to India in 1794, has gone down in history as the Father of Modern Missions. Yet there is another man of the same last name who was part of that great expansion of missions in the early nineteenth century. This "other Carey" in the history of foreign missions is less renowned than William Carey and other famous missionary heroes. Yet Lott Carey, a former slave in America, went as a pioneer missionary to Africa to help free that continent from enslavement to sin. His work on the western coast of Africa inspired a major African American effort in foreign missions and foreshadowed the spread of the gospel across that continent.

EARLY YEARS

Lott Carey was born around 1780 on a plantation in Charles City County, Virginia. As is the case with many slaves, little is known of his parents. Carey did maintain a fond memory of a godly grandmother. When he was a child, his grandmother told him of Africa and how people there did not know God. He asked, "And do all of them think that the great God lives far away from them and does not love them?" She replied that they needed to be told but that she was too old ever to tell them. "Son, you will grow strong," she told him. "You will lead many, and perhaps it may be you who will travel over the big seas to carry the great secret to my people."

There were many steps between that grandmother's wish and its fulfillment. The first step was taken in 1804 when Carey's master hired him out to work in the Richmond Tobacco Warehouse. At first, the change seemed to be for the worse. Although still enslaved, Carey found ample opportunity to get drunk, and he had enough "freedom of speech" to become well practiced in profanity. In that city, however, he heard the gospel at Richmond's First Baptist Church and was converted in 1807. The change in his life showed plainly as he became an excellent worker in the warehouse and was promoted to foreman.

After his conversion came a desire for learning. Like most slaves, Carey had never been taught to read and write. Listening to his pastor tell the story of Christ and Nicodemus from John 3, Carey felt a yearning to read that passage for himself—and the rest of the Bible as well. Painstakingly, he memorized passages of Scripture, then compared them with the printed words to figure out what they said. After learning to read, he spent all his spare moments at the warehouse reading. Carey also began attending a night school for blacks taught by a deacon at First Baptist Church.

Having found spiritual freedom in Christ, Carey was next able to secure freedom from physical enslavement. In 1813 he purchased his freedom and that of his two children for $850. Nothing is known of his first wife, but in 1815 he married for the second time. With the support of his new bride, Carey became an "exhorter" (lay preacher) among blacks. His skill and success impressed the white leaders of First Baptist Church, and they licensed him to preach. Another black preacher told a white minister, "I tell you I don't hear any of your white ministers that can preach like Lott Carey." Through God's blessing on his powerful, earnest sermons, Carey gathered a congregation of eight hundred.

A BURDEN FOR AFRICA

This ministry among Richmond's blacks led to Carey's involvement in foreign missions. While attending night school, Carey heard the report of a missionary tour of Africa. Much impressed, he said, "I have been determined for a long time to go to Africa and at least to see the country for myself." In 1815 he became secretary of the Richmond African Missionary Society, an organization designed to raise funds for work in Africa. The formation of this society, Carey said, made him wonder, "Am I satisfying God's requirement of me as a preacher of the Gospel? . . . Was my grandmother . . . right when she suggested, . . . 'perhaps it may be you who will travel over the big seas to carry the great secret to my people'?" Lott Carey believed that God would have him go to Africa to preach the "great secret" of the gospel.

Carey's interest in Africa arose during the time of America's first great surge of missionary effort. The country was in the midst of the Second Great Awakening, a great revival that brought spiritual renewal to the young nation. In churches, on college campuses, and on the frontier, thousands were finding new life in Christ.

The awakening also sparked a great push toward missions. During one of the college revivals, a group of students at Williams College in Massachusetts began to meet for prayer. During an outdoor prayer session in 1806, a thunderstorm drove the little group to the shelter of a haystack. As they waited out the storm, the students began to discuss the need for the gospel not just in America but around the world. *Someone* needed to take the gospel to other lands, they thought. Then one of them, Samuel J. Mills, said, "Why should *we* not be the ones? *We can do it if we will!*" Mills himself was never able to go to the field, but he founded a mission board and made trips abroad to scout out lands for foreign missions. (Mills wrote the report on Africa that caused Carey to express an interest in going to that continent.) Other missionary pioneers joined the cause, notably Adoniram Judson, the Baptist missionary to Burma who probably did more than any other man to confront the American church with the call of the mission field. And in the forefront of this wave of American Christians taking the gospel to foreign lands was Lott Carey.

Carey willingly explained his motives for wanting to go. Despite his work among the blacks of Richmond, Carey believed he could do more overseas. He saw mission work as an opportunity to serve God without running into the obstacle of racism that he had found in the United States. "I am an African, and in this country, however meritorious my conduct and respectable my character, I cannot receive the credit due to either," he said. "I wish to go to a country where I shall be estimated by my merits, not by my complexion; and I feel bound to labor for my suffering race." In his farewell sermon before leaving for Africa, he said,

> I am about to leave you, probably to see your faces no more. I am going to Africa, a land of heathenish darkness and degradation, to spread the light of salvation there. Jesus Christ commands me to go, and I must obey Him. I know not what may befall me, nor am I anxious about it. I may find a grave in the ocean, or among the savage men or beasts in the wilds of Africa. I long to preach the Gospel there to those who have never heard it. And I fear there may be thousands in this country who preach the Gospel, or profess obedience to Jesus Christ, who are not half awake to the magnitude of his requirements.

Carey challenged his hearers to share the burden that he felt. He described the final judgment and imagined Christ saying, "I commanded you to go into all the world, and preach the Gospel to every creature—have you obeyed me? Where have you been? Have you fulfilled the task I gave you, or have you sought your own ease and gratification, regardless of my commands?"

On May 1, 1819, the Baptist Board of Foreign Missions accepted Lott Carey as a candidate for the field. The tobacco warehouse immediately offered him a hefty raise to stay with the warehouse and not go to Africa. Carey refused. As he said shortly before leaving,

> This step is not taken to promote my own fortune, nor am I influenced by any sudden impulse. I have counted the cost and have sacrificed all my worldly possessions to this undertaking. I am prepared to meet imprisonment or even death in carrying out the purpose of my heart. It may be that I shall behold you no more on this side of the grave, but I feel bound to labor for my brothers, perishing as they are in the far distant land of Africa. For their sake and for Christ's sake I am happy in leaving all and venturing all.

There remained much preparation before going to Africa. Carey organized a congregation among the prospective settlers before he left, planning to transplant the church to Africa. Unfortunately, the Baptist mission board asked Carey to work with the American Colonization Society. Carey was not entirely pleased with this situation. The society sought to settle the problem of slavery in America by acquiring territory in Africa in which to resettle American blacks. The scheme was impractical to begin with, and many whites were much more interested in getting free blacks out of America than actually finding a way to end slavery. Carey feared—justifiably, as it turned out—that a secular organization so dedicated to solving the slavery problem would prove a poor vehicle for promoting the spread of the gospel. He wrote to the Baptist mission board, "If you intend doing anything for Africa you must not wait for the Colonization Society, nor for government, for neither of these are in search of missionary grounds, but of colonizing grounds; if it should not suit missionary needs, you cannot expect to gather in a missionary crop." His concerns, however, were not heeded.

AFRICA AT LAST

Finally, everything was ready. Carey and his small band of settlers sailed on January 23, 1821, for Sierra Leone, a British colony established on the western coast of Africa as a haven for freed blacks and rescued slaves. Just before his departure, Carey wrote to the General Convention of the Baptists that "we shall hoist our sails for Africa . . . with our bibles and our utensils, and our hopes in God our Savior."

The party landed in Freetown, Sierra Leone, in March. If Carey had any rosy dreams about the work he was undertaking, they were quickly shattered. The American Colonization Society had failed to purchase land in Africa for their colony. The missionary arrived, therefore, without official standing and without any means of support. Carey and the others worked for a time as farm laborers as they waited for their promised aid from America. Then a second, more serious trial occurred; Carey's wife became sick and died shortly after arrival. He was left now to raise his family alone.

Finally, in December 1821 the American Colonization Society "purchased" territory from the natives to form the colony of Liberia. (As part of the "negotiations" for the purchase, an American naval officer held a pistol to the head of an African chief to encourage him to sign the purchase agreement.) Carey moved there in 1822, hoping to begin his mission work in earnest. The limited number of settlers, however, and the daunting task they faced forced all the colonists to fill several roles. Carey was made "Health Officer and Government Inspector" and often functioned as a physician when disease afflicted the little colony. The governor, in fact, reported that Carey was forced to spend up to half of his time ministering to the sick.

The work was hard and often unrewarding. During the rough early days, Carey confronted one group of discouraged settlers and talked them out of returning to Sierra Leone. Some of the native tribes resented the establishing of the colony near their lands, and they harried it with raids. Carey compared the battles in building Liberia to those of Nehemiah and the children of Israel in rebuilding the walls of Jerusalem, even to the point of holding weapons close at hand as they worked. Yet he said, "There never has been an hour, or a minute, no, not even when the [bullets] were flying around my head, when I could wish myself again in America."

MINISTERING ON THE DARK CONTINENT

Most of Carey's mission work centered on the church he pastored in Monrovia, the capital of Liberia. His congregation was an interesting mixture. Carey ministered to immigrants from America, slaves rescued by the British from slave traders, and a handful of natives. It was among the Africans rescued by the British that Carey saw most of his few converts from the African tribal religions. The greater part of his increase came from black American immigrants. There were some scattered successes among the nearby natives, however. One native had heard a little of the gospel in Sierra Leone. Seeking a fuller understanding of Christ and the way of salvation, he traveled eighty miles to speak with Carey. The seeker was converted, and Carey baptized him and gave him his first communion. In halting English, the new convert gave his testimony:

> All the time my heart trouble me—all day—all night me can't sleep—by and by my heart grow too big—me fall down this time—now me can pray—me say Lord—have mercy. Then light come in my heart—make me glad—make me light—make me love the Son of God—make me love everybody.

By 1825 Carey had sixty members in his church, and he wrote, "The Lord has in mercy visited the settlement, and I have had the happiness to baptize nine . . . converts."

Carey also strove to promote education in Monrovia among both the colonists and the natives, but the lack of funds often hampered his work. He urged his brethren back home to send help: "O American Christians! Look this way! come this way! and help, if you cannot come! Send help for the Lord's sake! help Africa's sons out of the devil's bush into the kingdom of God; the harvest is already white." Eager to set an example, he even set up the Monrovia Mission Society among the Liberian Christians to raise money for missions.

Some American blacks opposed the Liberian work because it was associated with the American Colonization Society. They saw the work as mere camouflage for efforts to move free blacks from the United States. Carey took pains to distinguish his work from that of the society. He urged black Christians back home to support his work for the sake of the souls on the continent. "Africa suffers for gospel truth," he wrote, "and she will suffer, until missionaries can be sent, and settled in different parts of her continent." Just as William Carey saw his work in India as an opening to reach that whole subcontinent for Christ, Lott Carey saw Liberia as the starting point to carry the gospel to all of Africa.

Still, the burdens of government continued to interfere with Carey's work. He became the spokesman for a group of colonists who were dissatisfied with the way the governor of the colony, Jehudi Ashmun, was handling property disputes. The American Colonization Society ruled against Carey's faction, and the black missionary was forbidden even to preach for a time. He became reconciled to Ashmun, however, and in 1826 Carey was made assistant to the governor. When Ashmun left Liberia in March 1828 and died later that year, Carey became acting governor.

Carey did not long enjoy this honor. Trouble broke out again with one of the native tribes and with a slave trader. Carey began organizing the defense of the colony. He and several other colonists were preparing cartridges on November 8, 1828, when someone knocked a candle over into the gunpowder. The ensuing explosion fatally injured eight people. Among them was Carey, who died two days later.

HERITAGE

Lott Carey died after only a little more than eight years on the field. The results he had seen were, humanly speaking, small. But as is often the case with Christian work, Carey's heritage was far more extensive than he could have dreamed. In 1847 the colony of Liberia became an independent republic. It thus became the first republic in Africa and the only nation of that continent never to fall under colonial rule. Then in 1897 a group of black Christians in America founded the Lott Carey Foreign Mission Convention, a major missions agency of African American Baptists.

As important as Lott Carey was as a "founding father" of an African republic and as an inspiration to black American Christians, even more notable was his example to Christians of all races. Carey became the forerunner to Christian work across the continent of Africa. Just before Carey left the United States, he received a letter from a representative of the American Baptist Board of Foreign Missions. Quoting Psalm 68:31, the man wrote to the departing missionary, "Let nothing discourage you. Ethiopia shall stretch forth her hands unto God. You are engaged in the service of Him who can make the crooked straight, and the rough places plain." Neither that writer nor Carey himself fully realized the prophetic nature of those words. Africa indeed soon stretched out her hands unto God. Carey's dream "to spread the light of salvation" on that continent was not fulfilled in his brief lifetime. But the decades that followed saw thousands of missionaries and African preachers bringing, as Carey's grandmother called it, "the great secret" of salvation in Christ to the people of Africa.

For Further Reading

Fitts, Leroy. *Lott Carey: First Black Missionary to Africa.* Valley Forge, Pa.: Judson Press, 1978.

"Lott Cary." In *Annals of the American Pulpit,* edited by William B. Sprague. Vol. 6. Baptist. Reprint. New York: Arno Press, 1969, pp. 578-87.

Poe, William A. "Lott Cary: Man of Purchased Freedom." *Church History* 39 (1970): 49-61.

1812 TO 1901

July 4, 1839, Richmond, Virginia: the festive crowds in the Old Dominion's capital joyously celebrated the nation's sixty-third birthday. Jostled by the throng but not joining in the revels was a young black man. Although he stood over six feet tall, his spirit was bent with the weight of sin. "I was down in Capitol Square in Richmond," he said later. "Folks were swarming around and laughing and hurrahing when all of a sudden God's arrow of conviction went into my proud heart and brought me low. I left there badly crippled." Young John Jasper was on a journey that would take him from the obscurity of slavery to fame and prominence in his city, his state, and even his nation. More important, it would take him into service for God.

EARLY YEARS AND CONVERSION

John Jasper was born in 1812 on a plantation in Virginia, the youngest of twenty-four children. His father died two months before John's birth. It was his mother, a godly woman, who was the main influence in his life. Just before his death, Jasper recalled his mother: "She gave me to God before I was born, prayed me into glory when I was a wild reckless boy. Prayed me into preaching the Gospel." As a slave, John worked at whatever jobs he was told to do. As a boy, he was a house slave, waiting on his master's table. Later, as a field hand, he hoed and weeded under the hot Virginia sun. At the age of fifteen, John went to work in his master's tobacco warehouse, beginning by sweeping floors and gradually moving up to more skilled tasks. It was a life, perhaps, not greatly different from that of millions of other slaves in the southern United States before the Civil War.

Also like most other slaves, Jasper had no formal education. "I knowed nothing worth talking about concerning books," he said looking back in later years. "They was sealed mysteries to me, but I tell you I longed to break the seal." Then, when he was in his late twenties, Jasper was assigned to room with a slave who knew how to read a little. Jasper seized the opportunity.

> In the dead of the night he give me lessons outen the New
> York Spelling book. It was hard pulling, I tell you; harder on

him, for he knowed just a little, and it made him sweat to try to beat something into my hard head. It was worse with me. Up the hill every step, but when I got the light of the lesson into my noodle I fairly shouted, but I knowed I was not a scholar. The consequence was I crept along mighty tedious, getting a crumb here and there until I could read the Bible by skipping the long words, tolerable well. That was the start of my education—that is, what little I got.

Seven months after learning to read, John Jasper was converted to Christ. That miserable Fourth of July in Richmond had fallen in the middle of a period of deep conviction of sin. Jasper testified,

I was seeking God six long weeks—just because I was such a fool I couldn't see the way. . . . One July morning [in the tobacco warehouse] something happened. I was a tobacco-stemmer—that is, I took the tobacco leaf, and tored the stem out, and they weren't no one in that factory could beat me at that work. But that morning the stems wouldn't come out to save me, and I tored up tobacco by the pound and flung it under the table. Fact is, brethren, the darkness of death was in my soul that morning. My sins was piled on me like mountains; my feet was sinking down to regions of despair, and I felt that of all sinners I was the worst. I thought that I was going to die right then, and when I supposed it was my last breath, I flung up a cry, "Oh, Jesus, have mercy on me." Before I knowed it, the light broke; I was light as a feather; my feet was on the mountain; salvation rolled like a flood through my soul, and I felt as if I could knock off the factory with my shouts.

His shouts caught the attention of the factory overseer, who reported the matter to Jasper's master, Samuel Hardgrove, owner of the warehouse. Hardgrove, a Christian himself, called Jasper into his office and listened to him explain what had happened. Hardgrove surprised Jasper by shaking hands with him and saying, "John, I wish you mighty well. Your Saviour is mine, and we are brothers in the Lord." He gave Jasper permission to go about the warehouse testifying of his salvation and then gave him the rest of the day off to go tell anyone he wished about his experience.

For Jasper, this was the turning point of his life: "O happy day! Can I ever forget it? That was my conversion morning, and that day the Lord sent me out with the good news of the kingdom. For more than forty years I've been telling the story. My step is getting rather slow, my voice breaks down, and sometimes I am awful tired, but

81

still I'm telling it. My lips shall sing the dying love of the Lamb with my last expiring breath."

SLAVE PREACHER

Shortly after his conversion and baptism, John Jasper became a preacher and remained a slave preacher for twenty-five years. Being a slave preacher meant he could preach only with his master's permission and only when a white minister was present to observe and make sure that no "revolutionary" sentiments were voiced. Jasper often preached funeral sermons. Slave funerals were not mere formalities to be hurried through so that the dead could be buried. Rather, funerals were major social as well as religious events for slaves, much as the camp meeting was both a social and religious gathering on the frontier. Such slave funerals might even be held well after the deceased was buried and could last for hours. Jasper soon displayed natural gifts of eloquence that rapidly made him a funeral preacher much in demand.

Yet as a black and a slave, Jasper faced obstacles as he sought opportunities to preach the gospel. Jasper's master, Samuel Hardgrove, allowed him every fourth Sunday off for preaching, but he would allow him to preach on other Sundays only when the congregation could raise a dollar to pay for Jasper's lost time. A dollar was a large amount of money for slaves in the pre–Civil War South, and only those who really wanted Jasper could raise it. (Anything raised over the dollar, Hardgrove said, Jasper could keep.) On another occasion when Jasper arrived for a funeral, the white minister present was appalled to find that he was expected to share the service with a slave preacher. He therefore put Jasper out and conducted the service himself.

We know little of what John Jasper's early funeral sermons were like. No one thought to write them down when they were being preached. However, a funeral sermon Jasper gave years later, after he was free, may give us some idea of the flavor and form. He preached a double funeral for a man named William Ellyson and a woman named Mary Barnes. At the opening he said,

> Lemme say a word about this William Ellyson. I say it the first and get it off my mind. William Ellyson was no good man—he didn't say he was; he didn't try to be good, and they tell me he die as he live, without God and without hope in the world. It's a bad tale to tell on him, but he fix the story hisself. As the tree falls there must it lay. If you wants folks who

live wrong to be preached and sung to glory, don't bring them to Jasper. God comfort the mourner and warn the unruly.

> But, my brethren, Mary Barnes was different. She were washed in the blood of the Lamb and walked in white; her religion was of God. You could trust Mary anywhere; never catched her in them playhouses nor frisking in them dances; she wasn't no street-walker traipsing around at night. She loved the house of the Lord; her feet clung to the straight and narrow path; I knowed her. I seen her at the preaching, and seed her tending the sick and helping the mourning sinners. Our Sister Mary, good-bye. Your race is run, but your crown is sure.

Jasper preached much more than just funeral services. He spoke often in churches and served a long time as the "supply preacher" (virtually the pastor) in a church in Petersburg, Virginia. His master also gave him some leave to travel, and Jasper was able to hold meetings in nearby states. During the Civil War Jasper went into Richmond's hospitals to preach and to sing for the wounded Confederate soldiers there.

The end of the Civil War brought freedom to John Jasper. On the streets of Richmond he watched Ulysses S. Grant lead the victorious blue-coated troops into the city, and he rejoiced. He watched on another occasion in a downpour as the defeated Robert E. Lee rode by, and Jasper wept. He realized better than many the responsibility that came with freedom. When he saw a mob of newly freed blacks rioting at the close of the war, he cried out, "Richmond has fallen! We are free! But in the Name of God, let us act like men!"

EMANCIPATION AND A NEW MINISTRY

Now a free man, Jasper needed to find some way to make a living. He had only seventy-three cents to his name—along with forty-two dollars of debt. Devastated Richmond needed much labor to clear the wreckage and rebuild the city, and Jasper knew how to work. He got a job cleaning bricks from wrecked buildings, chipping away the old mortar so that they could be reused. "I'm just like Paul," he joked with his friends, "the preaching business got so bad he had to go back to tent-making." As he worked—earning fifty cents for each thousand bricks cleaned—he thought about the future.

Jasper wanted to continue to preach. But where, in this ruined city? And to whom? He left his brick-cleaning job in July and went to serve the church in Petersburg, where he had preached as a slave. But Jasper felt compelled to return to Richmond. He began holding services with nine members in a stable on an island in the James River. This meager handful eventually became the Sixth Mount Zion Baptist Church, a thriving church with room to hold nine hundred people but still lacking enough seats to hold the crowds that wanted in. Many white people, in fact, came to hear Jasper as his fame spread. They usually ended up in a "segregated" section in the balcony, and Jasper would joke, "Now, look'a here, you all white people, you keep over in your section. Don't get in the places of the regular customers."

People responded to John Jasper because he had the compassionate heart of a pastor. A member of his church, Virginia Adams, remembered: "Brother Jasper was the kindest man I reckon on the earth. You couldn't finish telling him about folks that was in trouble and want, before he'd be getting out his money. . . . Just tell him what was needed, and he begun to scratch in his pocket." Jasper did not share with others out of any great personal wealth. He apparently never took more than $62.50 a month in salary, and in the early days of the church he took nothing at all.

"Brother Jasper was none of your partial preachers," Virginia Adams recalled. "His church was his family, and he had no favorites. He did not bow down to the high nor hold himself above the low." Perhaps how he viewed others resulted from how he viewed himself before God: "He always thought of hisself as the servant of King Jesus. That was a slavery that he liked and never wished to get free from it."

His heart was large, but it was John Jasper's preaching that made him famous. He preached not only in his church but also wherever people would have him. His biographer records that Jasper was reported to have "preached in almost every county and city in Virginia." Some historians maintain that the total of those to whom he preached and the reported number of conversions from his meetings compare with those of notable evangelists of the day, such as Charles Finney.

Jasper's sermons were not unusually long, normally about fifty minutes in length. He described his method of preparing his sermons: "First, I read my Bible until a text gets hold of me. Then I go down to the James River and walk it in. Then I get into my pulpit and preach it out." His study was not formal, but it was thoroughly biblical. Despite his early illiteracy, Jasper had a remarkable knowledge of the Bible and was able to cite a multitude of verses from memory without error. One prominent white minister in Richmond went regularly to hear Jasper. Other whites protested. "The Negro's English is horrible," they said. "So it is," he replied, "but I do not go over to listen to Jasper's English. I go over to listen to Jasper talk about his Jesus."

The power of Jasper's sermons impressed hearers. "I stands before you today on legs of iron and none can stay me from preaching the Gospel of the Lord God," Jasper solemnly told his congregation. "I know well enough that the old devil is mad as a tempest about my being here; he know that my call to preach comes from God, and that's what makes him so mad when he see Jasper 'scend the pulpit, for he knows that the people is gwine to hear a message straight from heaven." Despite the fact that he never shed the dialect he had been speaking from his childhood, the images he presented through words were graphic and moving. He showed an uncanny ability to enthrall audiences by retelling the biblical narrative in his own memorable, penetrating style.

But John Jasper's sermons were not simply glorified storytelling. In the midst of the drama and sweep of his message was solid content of the gospel of salvation through Jesus Christ alone. This theme was constant in his sermons. At the conclusion of his sermon "Where Sin Come From," for example, Jasper said, "I just took time to tell where sin come from. But my tongue can't refuse to stop to tell you that the blood of the Lamb slain from the foundation of the world is greater than sin and mightier than hell. It can wash away our sins, make us whiter than the driven snow, dress us in redemption robes, bring us with shouts and hallelujahs back to that fellowship with our Father, that can never be broken long as eternity rolls."

Unlike many black preachers (particularly those in the North), Jasper was essentially conservative, concerned much more about preaching the gospel of salvation from sin than in any social reform: "This old time religion is not good enough for some folks in these last days. Some call this kind of talk foolishness, but if that be true then the Bible, and heaven, and these Christians' hearts, is full of that kind of foolishness. If this be old fogy religion, then I want my church crowded with old fogies." He sometimes clashed with more educated black preachers, who were embarrassed at his sometimes poor English. Yet one educated, more polished African American preacher admitted, "His preaching was more excitable than mine, and seemed to affect the people in a way that I could not."

"THE SUN DO MOVE"

John Jasper's most famous sermon was also his most controversial. A member of his church was arguing with another man
over whether the sun circled the earth or the earth circled the sun.
He then submitted the question to Pastor Jasper. The result was a
message Jasper first preached around 1878: "The Sun Do Move."
In an address some hour and a half in length, the preacher attempted to prove from the Scripture that the earth was flat and that
the sun indeed circled the earth. The sermon caused a sensation.
Most whites seemed more amused and amazed than offended.
Some who were Jasper's friends regretted the address. (Jasper's
main biographer says that he even considered omitting all mention
of the sermon from his book.) Many educated black preachers denounced the sermon, fearing it would reflect on their whole race.
Jasper was unapologetic. When others asked to hear the sermon, he
repeated it. In fact, he preached it over two hundred times before
his death. He delivered it at special announced services in his own
church; he went to other churches and cities and gave it there. One
promoter even set up a "lecture tour" of northern cities, including
Washington, Baltimore, and Philadelphia, where he repeated "The
Sun Do Move" many times. (Some audiences who came for enter-
tainment, however, were disappointed with the rather straightfor-
ward argument from the words of Scripture.) He became, at least
for a time, one of the most famous black preachers in America.

Jasper based his audacious claim on what he saw as the un-
questionable testimony of God's Word: "My God don't lie and He
ain't put no lie in the Book of eternal truth, and if I give you what
the Bible say, then I bound to tell the truth." For his first proof, the
preacher referred to the famous account in Joshua 10:8-14 of how
"the sun stood still in the midst of heaven, and hasted not to go
down about a whole day" (v. 13). "But what the Bible say?" Jasper
asked. "That's what I ask to know. It say that it was at the voice of
Joshua that it stopped. I don't say it stopped; tain't for Jasper to say
that, but the Bible, the Book of God, say so. But I say this; nothing
can stop until it has first started."

The preacher then turned to the narrative of King Hezekiah's
illness (II Kings 20:1-11; Isa. 38). As a sign of the king's healing,
God said, "Behold, I will bring again the shadow of the degrees,
which is gone down in the sun dial of Ahaz, ten degrees backward.
So the sun returned ten degrees, by which degrees it was gone
down" (Isa. 38:8). "Ain't that the movement of the sun?" asked
Jasper. "Bless my soul. Hezekiah's case beat Joshua. Joshua stop

the sun, but here the Lord make the sun walk back ten degrees; and yet they say that the sun stand stone still and never move a peg."

As a proof that the earth is flat, he referred to the "four angels standing on the four corners of the earth" (Rev. 7:1). "'Low me to ask if the earth is round, where do it keep its corners? A flat, square thing has corners, but tell me where is the corner of a apple, or a marble, or a cannon ball, or a silver dollar."

When he preached "The Sun Do Move," John Jasper demonstrated that he plainly did not understand the Copernican theory of the universe and that he was ignorant of astronomical science. Many Christians, believing as firmly in the inerrancy of the Bible as Jasper did, nonetheless understand that God accommodates His words to human figures of speech with phrases such as "the sun stood still" and "the four corners of the earth." But Jasper's critics missed the strength of the black preacher's message: no matter how you reconcile your language and astronomy, you must trust the Bible foremost. Jasper admitted that he was no scientist, nor did he have any personal interest in the question he was discussing: "'Low me, my friends, to put myself square about this movement of the sun. It ain't no business of mine whether the sun move or stand still, or whether it stop or go back or rise or set. All that is out of my hands entirely, and I got nothing to say. I got no theory on the subject. All I ask is that we will take what the Lord say about it and let His will be done about everything."

Unwavering faith in God's Word motivated John Jasper's stand. A critic of the sermon argued with the preacher and warned him that he was going to harm all other African Americans with his views. Jasper recalled his reply to the critic: "I tell him John Jasper ain't set up to be no scholar, and don't know the philosophies, and ain't trying to hurt his people, but is working day and night to lift them up, but his foot is on the rock of eternal truth. There he stands and there he is going to stand till Gabriel sound the judgment note." He said to his critics, "When you ask me to stop believing in the Lord's Word and to pin my faith to your words, I ain't a gwine to do it. I take my stand by the Bible and rest my case on what it says."

FINAL YEARS

Late in his life Jasper once said, "Comparatively speaking, my time in this world is skin deep, and I look at my hand and think how thin the skin is, and I feel that sure enough he must soon be going." Yet even as he knew his days were winding down, Jasper continued his fervent pulpit ministry. In one sermon he imagined a taunting scorner asking, "Well, Jasper, have you got any religion to give away?" Then he answered, "I'se free to say that I ain't got as much as I want. For forty-five years I been begging for more, and I ask for more in this trying hour. But, bless God, I'se got religion to give away. The Lord have filled my hands with the Gospel, and I stand here to offer free salvation to any that will come. If in this big crowd there is one lost sinner that have not felt the cleansing touch of my Savior's blood, I ask him to come today and he shall never die."

John Jasper passed away in 1901, still preaching up to within days of his death. People often speak of a man "going to his reward" when he dies. Jasper himself portrayed something of those rewards in a sermon in which he imagined himself walking the streets of heaven: "Look there; mighty sweet house, ain't it lovely? Look there; see that on the door; hallelujah, it's John Jasper. Said He was gwine to prepare a place for me; there it is! Too good for a poor sinner like me, but He built it for me, a turn-key job, and mine forever. Oh, what must it be to be there!" Then, stepping back mentally from that prepared home, Jasper delivered what could have been his farewell as he departed life: "And now, friends, if you'll 'scuse me, I'll take a trip to the throne and see the King in his royal garments. Oh, what it must be to be there!"

For Further Reading

Day, Richard Ellsworth. *Rhapsody in Black: The Life Story of John Jasper.* Philadelphia: Judson Press, 1953.

Fant, Clyde E., and William M. Pinson, Jr. "John Jasper." In *20 Centuries of Great Preaching.* Vol. 4. *Newman to Robertson.* Waco: Word Books, 1971, pp. 226-57.

Hatcher, William E. *John Jasper: The Unmatched Negro Philosopher and Preacher.* 1908. Reprint. New York: Negro Universities Press, 1969.

DANIEL PAYNE

1811 TO 1893

In 1852 the Reverend Charles Avery, founder of a school for blacks in Allegheny, Pennsylvania, addressed an assembly of the African Methodist Episcopal (AME) Church. One member of the denomination rose afterwards and thanked Avery for his words: "We are sensible of the fact that if we are ever elevated to the rights and privileges of American citizens we must become an educated people." He went on to exhort his fellow African Americans, saying, "Let every minister, therefore, among us educate himself! Let every mother and father educate their sons and daughters. Then, as water rises to its natural level, so will we rise to the position destined by reason and heaven." The speaker was Daniel Payne, a minister in the AME Church, a future bishop of that church, and a man who himself did much to promote education among blacks in the nineteenth century.

Christians have long recognized the value of education as a tool in God's service. The Puritans who founded New England, for example, adopted the "Old Deluder Satan" Act in 1647. "It being one chief project of the old deluder, Satan, to keep men from the knowledge of the Scriptures," the act said, the colonists were required to establish schools "that learning may not be buried in the graves of our fathers."

Payne recognized how education better equipped the servant of God. But he also saw Christianity as the source of true education, an education that would uplift both man and society. "Christianity is an educating power," he said. "It educates in every direction that touches humanity; not religiously only, but morally also; not morally only, but intellectually also; not intellectually only, but, because it is a religious, moral, and intellectual educational power, it logically affects and modifies all the forms of civil and political life." Payne believed that the black race needed Christ above all. But he also believed that it needed education to take its rightful place in American society. And a Christian education was the best possible education they could have. Christ-centered education was the burden of Daniel Payne.

89

EARLY YEARS

Daniel Alexander Payne was born to free black parents on February 24, 1811, in Charleston, South Carolina. His parents were devout Methodists, naming him after the prophet Daniel and dedicating him to the Lord from birth. As a child, young Daniel joined in the regular family worship. Then when Payne was four years old, his father died, and his mother died only a few years later. After his mother's death Payne went to a black orphanage school for two years; was apprenticed to a shoe merchant for a year; was apprenticed to his brother-in-law, a carpenter, for four and a half years; and then worked nine months as a tailor. While working for the carpenter, Payne was inspired by a biographical sketch of John Brown of Haddington, a Scottish Presbyterian pastor and writer. Payne was particularly impressed at how Brown had taught himself to read the ancient languages. "If Brown learned Latin, Greek, and Hebrew without a living teacher," Payne asked himself, "why can't I?" Therefore, he began to read everything he could find.

In his autobiography, *Recollections of Seventy Years,* Payne made no mention of one major event in black history that took place in Charleston during his childhood years. The Reverend Morris Brown built in the city a large and flourishing congregation for the African Methodist Episcopal Church, an independent black denomination based in the North. By 1817 the membership numbered one thousand. Among Brown's members was a former slave named Denmark Vesey. Apparently unknown to Brown, Vesey and some other blacks in Charleston planned a slave rebellion. The plot was discovered, and Vesey and thirty-four others were executed. A mob burned down the church and the state exiled Morris Brown and most of the other leaders of the church from South Carolina. The Vesey plot fanned white fears of slave revolts and made them suspicious of the activities of free blacks in Charleston.

Payne, however, appears to have been little affected by these events at first. Even though his parents were dead, Payne continued faithfully to attend church. (Like his parents, he went to a church in the large, white-controlled Methodist denomination, not the AME church.) He became seriously concerned about his soul when he was fifteen, and he was converted when he was eighteen. That conversion came while he was attending a series of special prayer meetings that his church was holding to pray for revival. He wrote, "Here I too gave him my *whole heart,* and instantly felt that peace which passeth all understanding and that joy which is unspeakable and full of glory." Shortly after his conversion, Payne felt a call to a specific ministry: "Several weeks after this event, between twelve and one o'clock one day, I was in my humble chamber, pouring out my prayers into the listening ears of the Saviour, when I felt as if the hands of a man were pressing my two shoulders and a voice speaking within my soul saying: *'I have set thee apart to educate thyself in order that thou mayest be an educator to thy people.'* The impression was *irresistible* and *divine;* it gave a new direction to my thoughts and efforts."

With this new conviction driving him, Payne pursued his private study with even more enthusiasm. He made items with the carpentry skills he had learned and then sold the items to buy books. He quickly bolted down his food so that he could spend the rest of his breakfast and lunch hours reading. After work, Payne read until midnight and then arose at 4:00 A.M. to read by candlelight until he began work at 6:00. Finally, his learning reached a point where he felt he could pursue his dream—starting his own school.

THE FIRST SCHOOL

Payne opened his school in Charleston in 1829 with three children who paid fifty cents a month and three adults who paid the same amount to attend night classes. Understandably, Payne barely got by financially. While struggling to teach and live at the same time, he received a tempting offer. A well-to-do white man on his way to the West Indies offered Payne the chance to go with him as an assistant. "If you will go with me," he said, "the knowledge that you will acquire of men and things will be of far more value to you than the wages I will pay you. Do you know what makes the difference between the master and the slave? *Nothing but superior knowledge.*" Payne refused the offer, thinking to himself, "If it is true that there is nothing but superior knowledge between the master and the slave, I will not go with you, but will rather go and obtain that knowledge which constitutes the master."

In order to teach his students, he had to teach himself. Payne diligently learned Greek, French, and Latin. The study of science and nature in his school was definitely "hands on." Payne caught animals such as snakes, cleaned them, stuffed them, and displayed them in his school. "I bought a live alligator," Payne recalled, "made one of my pupils provoke him to bite, and whenever he opened his mouth, I discharged a load of shot from a small pistol down his throat. As soon as he was stunned, I threw him on his back, cut his throat, ripped his chest, hung him up and studied his viscera till they ceased to move." His search for knowledge sometimes proved dangerous. In 1832 he damaged his sight permanently by watching an eclipse without any protection for his eyes.

Payne's school grew until it became the largest for blacks in the city (about sixty students). But in 1831 Nat Turner, a slave preacher in Virginia, led a slave rebellion that eventually resulted in the deaths of about sixty whites and a hundred blacks. It was like the Vesey plot, only worse, for this time violence had actually erupted. Frightened by the revolt, legislatures across the South began passing laws to make sure such uprisings did not occur again, and educated slaves were considered one source of "dangerous ideas." In 1834 South Carolina passed a law forbidding anyone to teach a slave to read and write. Furthermore the law prohibited free blacks not only from teaching slaves but even from teaching other free blacks how to read and write. The penalty for a white man convicted under the law was a sentence of up to six months in prison and a fine of one hundred dollars. The penalty for a free black was a fifty-dollar fine and fifty lashes with a whip. Faced with this law, Payne closed his school on March 31, 1835, after five years of operation.

Payne decided to leave the South rather than give up his dream of education. As he prepared to depart, a friend, a white clergyman, wrote, "Pursue knowledge wherever it is to be found. Like the air you breathe, it may be inhaled everywhere; like gold, it passes current among all classes. *God is on the side of virtue.*" He left Charleston on May 9, 1835, and went to New York. Payne wrote, "Every night for many years after I left Charleston did I dream about it—wandering over its streets, bathing in its rivers, worshiping in its chapels, or teaching in my school-room." He left his only sister in Charleston and never saw her again.

EARLY YEARS IN THE NORTH

Payne arrived in New York with letters of introduction to Methodist, Congregational, and Episcopal clergymen. Each told him in turn that he should go to Africa. A Lutheran, however, was impressed with Payne and told him about the Society of Inquiry on Missions, a student organization desiring to sponsor a black to be educated at Gettysburg Theological Seminary, a Lutheran school in Pennsylvania. Payne was unsure. He really did not plan to become a minister but wanted to be a teacher. His friend replied that he would not be required to be a minister and added, "And if you should not enter the ministry, your training in theology will make you more useful in the school-room."

Payne tremendously enjoyed his studies at Gettysburg; it was what he had dreamed of in South Carolina. But his life was not all academics. In his personal journal for October 1835 he recorded these resolutions: "I will be in bed every night at 10 o'clock. I will arise every morning 4 o'clock. I will devote a hour directly after rising from bed to prayer, reading the scriptures and meditation. Directly after dinner I will devote another hour to the same purpose, at sunset ditto, and one hour before retiring to bed, ditto, so that 4 hours of each day shall be spent in my studies and recreation. O Lord, thou knowest my weakness. I pray thee give me fortitude to practice these resolutions which I make tonight." Likewise on November 6, 1836, he wrote, "Now, O Lord God of Heaven and Earth, to Thee I present my soul, body and Spirit with all their blood redeemed powers, a living sacrifice holy and acceptable which is my reasonable service. Take the offering and sanctify it to thy use and thy glory for my Redeemer's sake. Amen."

While in seminary, Payne also mixed "practical" work with his academic preparation. He held a Sunday school for black children in the area, and he occasionally preached in special meetings. His journal for April 5, 1837, revealed his burden: "Yesterday my soul was drawn out to mourn and pray over the moral desolutions of my kinsmen according to the flesh in this village and its vicinity, great are the ravages which sin is making in our midst. O Lord, send us help from thy throne!"

Unfortunately, his eye problem from watching the eclipse cropped up again. After only two years, he was forced to drop out before completing his course. Payne was despondent until God comforted him through Matthew 13:16—"But blessed are your eyes, for they see: and your ears, for they hear."

By now, Payne's doubts about the ministry were gone, and he prepared to take his first pastorate. Although he had attended a Lutheran seminary, he found opportunities available in several denominations. A close friend recommended that he consider the African Methodist Episcopal Church. Payne was uncomfortable with the AME Church, however. He had heard of rumors about its uneducated ministers, how preachers bragged that they had never gone to college or had never studied Latin, Greek, or Hebrew. Therefore, Payne took the pulpit of a Presbyterian church in East Troy, New York, in 1837.

His stay with that church, however, was relatively short. During a New Year's Eve service, he became so involved with preaching and counseling all night that he strained his throat. Payne not only lost his voice for a year but also suffered an illness that kept him in bed for six months. Realizing that he could not continue in the pastorate, he resigned his pulpit. After a period of rest and recovery, he moved to Philadelphia, where he taught school from 1839 to 1843.

THE AFRICAN METHODIST EPISCOPAL CHURCH

In Philadelphia, Payne overcame his initial doubts and joined the African Methodist Episcopal Church in 1841. Exposed to the work of the AME Church firsthand, Payne became convinced that as part of that denomination he could serve God best. He first served as the pastor of a church in Washington, D.C. Since slavery still existed there, he, as a free black, had to undergo the humiliation of depositing a thousand dollars to guarantee his "good behavior" in the city. In 1845 he moved to a church in Baltimore. While living in that city he married, but his wife died in childbirth within a year. The child, a daughter, died nine months later. All the while, Payne suffered through conflicts with the trustees of his church over matters such as selling some church property to another AME congregation. (Payne wanted to be generous to the other church, but others wanted the full amount the property was worth.) When he and the denomination expelled some members, one angry woman attacked him with a club, but he was not seriously injured.

Disturbed by the poor educational background of AME ministers, Payne in 1844 and 1845 wrote five "Epistles on the Education of the Ministry." He simply called for higher educational standards for ministers, but he nearly split the denomination. Some considered it "unspiritual" to have educated ministers. When he saw the controversy he was causing, Payne thought he would drop the matter for the sake of peace. But Bishop Morris Brown (the minister driven out of Charleston by the Denmark Vesey affair) wanted to see reforms enacted. He and other AME leaders persuaded the denomination to adopt a plan for a course of private study. However, adoption of the program did no good. Payne lamented that because of "lack of unity in purpose and oneness in action, and because we were all too poor to assume individual responsibility, the project was abandoned."

Nonetheless, Payne impressed the leadership of the AME Church. In 1852 he was elected a bishop. Never a physically strong man, Payne was not sure that he was up to the rigors of the job. He said, "I prayed earnestly that God would take away my life rather than allow me to be put into an office for which I felt myself so utterly unfit." Rather than prove "unfit," Payne proved one of the most dynamic leaders in the group's history.

The office of bishop was certainly one that brought problems along with prestige. One of the first major tests to face Bishop Payne involved a white woman in Philadelphia who in 1853 opened a school for blacks. Other whites shunned her for working with blacks, so she worshiped in an AME church. However, several women in the church began to pressure the pastor to expel her because she was white. Their families threatened to withhold their offerings to the church and starve out both Bishop Payne and the pastor if they did not agree. Payne stood firm, but the pastor gave in and expelled the woman. Afterwards, Bishop Payne used his authority to deny this pastor another church. The infuriated minister confronted Payne, shook his fist at him, and said, "You dare to leave me without an appointment on account of that white woman! Open your mouth if you dare, and I will lay you flat upon the floor." He left in rage. Payne would not revoke his decision: "I believed that the pastor who would turn away from God's sanctuary any human being on account of color was not fit to have charge of a gang of dogs."

ABOLITION

In the 1830s sentiment to abolish slavery was stirring the country. Earlier in American history, some reformers had suggested that the nation might end slavery through colonization, sending the blacks to Africa. That effort failed because most blacks saw themselves as Americans and did not wish to go to Africa. Also many blacks suspected with good reason that some of the reformers were more interested in getting free blacks out of the country than in freeing slaves. Other reformers suggested a policy of gradual emancipation. By this they meant that legislation should set time limits to free slaves and their children over a period of years. Many Northern states, such as Pennsylvania, had abolished slavery in this manner. The most popular view in the North, however, came to be that of *immediate* emancipation—the freeing of all the slaves at once, and the sooner, the better. A wide range of reformers supported this view. Liberal Unitarian William Lloyd

Garrison and his newspaper, *The Liberator,* called for immediate emancipation. So did evangelical Christians such as evangelist Charles Finney and Theodore Weld, one of Finney's converts who became an effective spokesman for the abolitionist cause.

When he arrived from South Carolina, Payne believed in gradual emancipation because he thought blacks should be educated first to prepare them for freedom. Then he met Christian businessman and abolitionist Lewis Tappan. On hearing Payne's views, Tappan asked him, "Don't you know that men can't be educated in a state of slavery?" The question started Payne thinking, and in a short time he came to believe in immediate emancipation. In fact, he became so eloquent in his call for freeing the slaves that a major antislavery society offered to make him its paid representative to travel around the country and speak against slavery. Payne wholeheartedly supported the organization's goals, but he felt it would be wrong to turn from the pulpit ministry to which he had committed himself. Payne asked the advice of a friend who said, "I think God has called you to the pulpit, and therefore I advise that you stick to theology and the work of the Christian Ministry." He therefore declined the offer, but he continued to work in behalf of abolition, including work as a leader of a committee in Philadelphia that helped runaway slaves.

One can see Payne's views on slavery clearly in an address he gave in 1839 to a Lutheran synod meeting. He urged them to adopt a report condemning slavery. He argued on humanitarian grounds: *"American Slavery brutalizes man—destroys his moral agency, and subverts the moral government of God."* He added, "I am opposed to slavery, not because it enslaves the black man, but because it enslaves *man.* And were all the slaveholders in this land men of color, and the slaves white men, I would be as thorough and uncompromising an abolitionist as I now am." He pointed out the cruelties of slavery—families broken up at an owner's whim, the mockery of the institution of marriage, and more.

Payne also argued from religious grounds. He declared, "Thus saith the Son of God, 'Search the Scriptures.' Does not slavery seal up the word of God, and make it criminal for the slave to read it?" He related incidents from his days in South Carolina. On one occasion, a slave licensed to preach by the Methodist church had a fruitful ministry on some of the plantations. Then a patrol caught him "and whipped him in the most cruel manner, and compelled him to promise that he would never return again to preach to those slaves." At another time, Payne himself joined a group of blacks who were preaching to poor white farmers who had never heard the gospel. After four Sundays they had seen some fruit, including one ill farmer who found Christ before he died. Then the patrols came in and put an end to this work—forbidding free blacks to preach the gospel even to whites. Payne said that only a few days before the meeting he had talked to a runaway slave staying in Payne's home on his way to freedom. Payne asked the man whether he were a Christian. "No sir," the man replied, "white men treat us so bad in Mississippi that we can't be Christians."

When the Civil War broke out, Payne was minister of a church in Washington, D.C. With the Southern states out of the Union, Congress passed a law abolishing slavery in the District of Columbia. Some advisers to President Lincoln urged him to veto the bill. They feared it might drive slave-holding states still in the Union (such as Kentucky and Missouri) to the Confederate side. Lincoln gave no indication of what he would do. Payne was able to make an appointment with the president on April 11, 1862. The black pastor reminded Lincoln that before he left Springfield, Illinois, he had asked for people to pray for him. Payne then added that the black people of the Union had been among those praying most fervently for him and his cause. Lincoln listened and replied, "Well, I must believe that God has led me thus far, for I am conscious that I never would have accomplished what has been done if he had not been with me to counsel and to shield."

Lincoln still would not say what he would do with the bill, but he signed it five days later (probably as he had intended to do all along). The black churches of Washington invited Payne to preach a thanksgiving sermon. In that message, entitled "Welcome to the Ransomed of the Lord," Payne said, "We are gathered to celebrate the emancipation, yea, rather, the *Redemption* of the enslaved people of the District of Columbia." Noting the responsibility that freedom brings, he warned them against "indolence, . . . vice, licentiousness, and crime" in favor of "a well-regulated liberty." True liberty, he said, could not come without Christ.

> We invite you to our Churches, because we desire you to be religious; to be more than religious; we urge you *to be godly*. We entreat you to never be content until you are emancipated from sin, from sin without, and from sin within you. But this kind of freedom is attained only through the faith of Jesus, love for Jesus, obedience to Jesus. As certain as the American Congress has *ransomed* you, so certain, yea, more certainly has Jesus redeemed you from the guilt and power of sin by his own precious blood.

As you are now free in body, so now seek to be free in soul and spirit, from sin and Satan. The *noblest freeman is he whom Christ makes free.*

He stressed, as always, the importance of education. *"Rest not till you have learned to read the Bible,"* he urged. Furthermore, he said, "Keep your children in the schools, even if you have to eat less, drink less and wear coarser raiments; though you eat but two meals a day, purchase but one change of garment during the year, and relinquish all of the luxuries of which we are so fond." Above all, he urged the ransomed to pray—"To make prayers, intercessions, supplications, thanksgivings for national authorities . . . *is a command from heaven.* Obey it, and you shall be blessed—always do it, and you shall be made a blessing to others. Whom God has blessed no man can curse."

In May 1865, with the war just over, Payne visited Charleston for the first time in thirty years. "Destruction marked every square through which we passed," he wrote. "The holes made in the walls of the finest warehouses and residences; the burned, ruined walls of the Circular and Cumberland Churches—all showed the devastating hand of war." Peace had come, but the city had to be rebuilt. Likewise, slavery was dead, but there was still much to do. Payne said on one occasion, "Freedom is one thing; qualification is another. The former only places us in a position to obtain the latter, but it is no substitute for it." Freedom had come to all blacks; now Payne saw that he must concentrate on the "qualifications" that would enrich freedom.

WILBERFORCE UNIVERSITY

Payne married again in 1854, to a widow with three children. They were living in Cincinnati, but fearing the "corrupting influences" of the city, they sought a better environment to raise their children. Eventually, they moved to Tawawa Springs near Xenia, Ohio. He did not know it at the time, but Payne had come to the site of his greatest ministry—Wilberforce University.

The Methodist Episcopal Church, North, a large, dominantly white group, opened Wilberforce University in Tawawa Springs (later renamed Wilberforce) in October 1856 as a school for blacks. The name Wilberforce was appropriate, for English statesman and evangelical Christian William Wilberforce had led the fight to abolish slavery within the British Empire. The school did well until the Civil War caused a huge drop in enrollment. The resulting financial pressures forced the school to close in June 1862.

In 1863 the Methodists asked Payne, who was one of the original trustees, if he were willing to buy the fifty-two-acre property for the AME Church by paying the $10,000 debt. The state of Ohio wanted to buy the site for an asylum.The bishop had to decide without being able to wait for the meeting of the annual conference of the AME Church. Although Payne had only $10, he, nonetheless, seized the opportunity and agreed. He was elected president of Wilberforce, and through the generous giving of the church was able to raise $7,500 by 1865. The work showed every sign of prospering.

April 14, 1865, has gone down in infamy as the day that Abraham Lincoln was shot. For the faculty and students of Wilberforce University, it was a day of double tragedy. That day most of the students and staff had gone to nearby Xenia to join in a celebration over the fall of Richmond to the Union forces. President Payne was on a trip in Baltimore. Only one staff member was on campus when an arsonist struck. The main building, the heart of the Wilberforce campus, went up in a blaze. "Our dormitories, recitation rooms, library and chapel were all consumed," Payne recalled, "and our school almost broken up. We had to begin anew."

Looking at the charred ashes of their dreams, Payne and the others refused to quit. They began by holding classes in a cottage. The school managed to get a replacement building open and in use by 1868, but it was not actually finished until 1876. By 1873, Payne said, the property was worth $60,000 and had a debt of only $414. The school was preparing students for careers in teaching, law, medicine, the Christian ministry, and other fields. "But above all," Payne said in an annual report, "scores of young men and women have been brought to a saving knowledge of the truth in Christ Jesus within the halls of the institution." Eventually the campus was also the site of a seminary—appropriately named Payne Theological Seminary.

Daniel Payne set out what he saw as the true philosophy of education for Wilberforce or any other Christian institution: "I do mean a Christian education, that which draws out head and heart towards the Cross, while after consecrating them to the Cross, sends the individuals from beneath the Cross with the spirit of Him who died upon it; sends them abroad well fitted for Christian usefulness, a moral, a spiritual power, moulding, coloring community, and preparing it for a nobler and higher state of existence in that world where change never comes."

RAISING THE STANDARDS

Payne retired as president of Wilberforce in 1876. He was sixty-five years old and not in the best of health. Payne was a small man to begin with, and poor health kept him under a hundred pounds for the last forty years of his life. Yet he had many goals he still wished to pursue and did not intend to let advancing age or illness stop him. He had been commissioned in 1848 to write a history of the AME Church, and he had been researching the work all the while. Even with his retirement from Wilberforce, the book was not actually published until 1891 because the bishop stayed so busy.

Daniel Payne, having lived under slavery and through the Civil War, was determined to lift up his people, particularly those in the African Methodist Episcopal Church. He took as his standard for this work the Word of God: "An individual man or woman must never follow conviction in regard to moral, religious, civil, or political questions until they are first tested by the unerring word of God. If a conviction infringes upon the written word of God, or in any manner conflicts with that word, the conviction is not to be followed. It is our duty to abandon it."

The general illiteracy of the rank-and-file AME membership was a burden to Payne. He noted, "A glance over the congregation of Bethel [Church in Philadelphia] will convince you of this; for in an audience from one to two thousand souls, you cannot see one hundred using our hymn-books." Most did not use them for the very good reason that they could not read.

Payne also wanted to draw his church away from shallow emotionalism. For example, he sternly denounced "the ring." This was a practice in some AME revival services in which a circle of believers gathered around a repentant sinner and sang and clapped until the man or woman claimed to be converted. A defender of the practice said, "Sinners won't get converted unless there is a ring." Payne replied, "You might sing till you fell down dead, and you would fail to convert a single sinner, because nothing but the Spirit of God and the word of God can convert sinners."

Payne also wanted to improve the quality of music in the churches. He was one of the first pastors in his denomination to use a church choir, and he also wrote a few hymns. The bishop strongly opposed what he called "cornfield ditties," emotional, trivial songs with little biblical content. (Payne offered a sample of a "cornfield ditty": "I was way over there where the coffin fell; / I heard that sinner as he screamed in hell.")

100

It was the ministers, however, for whom Payne felt the greatest burden. At times, the resistance of the clergy of his church to education frustrated the bishop. He spoke on one occasion of how the AME Church sent preachers out "to do what? I ask again, to do what? You say to preach the Gospel. What Gospel? The Gospel of Christ? Well, do they? No! They preach what is in no Bible under heaven. . . . Rant, obscene language, rude and vulgar expressions. Irreverent exclamations, empty . . . nonsense, and the essence of superstition, constitute the gospel they preach." In an address given in 1852, Payne discussed not only the problems with the denomination's preaching but also his solution: "Some there are who believe it [preaching] to consist in loud declamation and vociferous talking; some in whooping stamping and beating the Bible or desk with their fists, and in cutting as many odd capers as a wild imagination can suggest; and some err so grievously on this subject as to think that he who hallooes the loudest and speaks the longest is the best preacher." He urged ministers to pursue education, using as their model "our Lord and Master Jesus Christ the Righteous— his head was all knowledge, and his heart all holiness. He was as free from ignorance as he was free from sin. God grant that we may all seek to be like him as much in the one case as in the other."

Just three years before his death, Payne gave an ordination sermon for new bishops of the AME Church. In that sermon he said, "Do not try to set race against race. That is the work of the devil, not of Christ. You must not set the white man against the black man, nor the brown man against the yellow man; but harmonize them all, and teach them to walk in peace. It is your work to teach the gospel of the Lord Jesus Christ—that he died for all. You must try to save all, and make all love in one common brotherhood." Payne died on November 29, 1893, at his home in Wilberforce, Ohio. He had come a long way from the small boy who rode on his father's shoulders along the streets of Charleston, South Carolina. He had made a lasting impact, a *national* impact, through his work for abolition, education, black dignity, and the preaching of the gospel.

For Further Reading

Coan, Josephus R. *Daniel Alexander Payne—Christian Educator.* Philadelphia: The A.M.E. Book Concern, 1935.

Payne, Daniel. *Recollections of Seventy Years.* 1888. Reprint. New York: Arno Press and the New York Times, 1968.

Steumpfle, Herman G. "Daniel Alexander Payne as Hymn Writer." *The Hymn,* 29-31.

Many African American Christians have gone to Africa, the land of their heritage, to carry the gospel to that continent. David George and Lott Carey worked in Sierra Leone and Liberia, respectively, serving as brave pioneers for the gospel when the modern missions movement was young. Other black missionaries followed. Seeing the work of these missionaries—and white ones as well—some Christians expectantly quoted Psalm 68:31, "Ethiopia shall soon stretch out her hands unto God." They envisioned God turning the continent to Christ, and they saw black missionaries in particular as one of the means He would use.

But in the midst of this wave of Americans going to Africa, there was one African who came to America. The account of his journey to America was one of drama and adventure, and the story of his brief life in this country was one of inspiration and determination. This remarkable young man was Samuel Morris.

AN AFRICAN PRINCE

Samuel Morris was born as Kaboo of the Kru tribe in Ivory Coast in 1873. He was the son of a chief (hence a prince), but his father was only one of many competing rulers in the region, and a minor one at that. His tribe usually suffered in tribal warfare, and Kaboo in particular bore the brunt of the defeats. Twice after his father lost wars, Kaboo was held hostage, or "put into pawn," until his father paid the ransom. The second time that Kaboo was put into pawn, when he was about fifteen years old, was more harrowing. His father could not raise sufficient ransom to satisfy the victors. The conquering chief ordered Kaboo whipped daily with a thorny vine in front of a witness who then carried word of this treatment to Kaboo's father to "encourage" him to come up with the ransom. "This cruel man whipped me every day," the captive later recalled. "He whipped me without any cause, and every day the whipping got harder and harder."

Kaboo's back became raw from the torture, and he became feverish from infection. Furthermore, if his father was unable to raise sufficient ransom, Kaboo's captors would make an example of him by burying him in the ground up to his neck for the ants to eat. Finally, during one of his daily beatings, Kaboo suddenly broke free. He plunged into the jungle before his astonished tormentors could stop him. Hiding in a tree until after dark, he then began to work his way through the jungle. He could not go home, for as an escaped hostage, he would put his father and his whole village in danger of retaliation. Therefore, he moved on toward the seacoast, hiding in trees by day to escape pursuit and traveling by night.

Eventually Kaboo arrived at a coffee plantation near Monrovia, Liberia. He found a fellow member of the Kru tribe working on the plantation and got a job there. He also heard Christian missionaries for the first time. Christian devotion both puzzled and interested him. Once Kaboo saw his Kru friend praying. When asked what he was doing, the man said, "I am talking to God."

"Who is God?" asked Kaboo.

"He is my Father," came the reply.

"Then, you are talking to your Father," observed Kaboo. (After he was converted, he always referred to praying as "talking to my Father.") He attended the services with great interest. A lady missionary taught him English as she taught him the Bible. Kaboo continued praying, even agonizing over his sense of sinfulness. He prayed out loud in bed—so much so that his bunkmates in the bunkhouse on the plantation threatened to throw him out. Kaboo then started going out to the jungle to pray. Returning to bed one night after midnight, he found peace in dramatic fashion. He recalled later,

> I went to my bunk, weary and heavyhearted, and lay down to rest. My tongue was still, but my heart went on praying. All at once my room grew light! At first I thought the sun was rising, but the others all around me were sound asleep. The room grew lighter till it was full of glory. The burden of my heart suddenly disappeared and I was filled with a sense of inner joy.
>
> My body felt as light as a feather. I was filled with a power that made me feel that I could almost fly. I could not contain my joy but shouted until everyone in the barracks was awakened. There was no more sleep there that night. Some thought I had gone crazy; others, that a devil had gotten into me. But I knew my own heart. This was my adoption. I was now a son of the heavenly King. I knew that my Father had saved me for a purpose, and that He would work with me.

ACROSS THE SEA

After his conversion, Kaboo was baptized and took a new name, "Samuel Morris," to symbolize his new birth. (The name was that of a supporter and friend of the missionary who had helped lead him to Christ.) He lived two more years in Liberia doing various jobs and becoming a faithful supporter of mission work, particularly in his prayers, at which he sometimes spent hours at a time. He told the missionaries that he was interested in preaching to his people. They encouraged him to go to America, be educated, and then return prepared to preach.

In addition to education, Samuel Morris found another reason for going to America. As he listened to the missionaries, Morris became very interested in the Bible's teaching concerning the Holy Spirit. He constantly bombarded one missionary, Lizzie MacNeil, with questions about the Holy Spirit. She answered them as fully as she could until finally she said, "If you want to know any more you must go to Stephen Merritt . . . ; he told me all I know of the Holy Ghost."

"I am going," Morris said, "where is he?"

The missionary told him that Merritt lived in New York, where he was a minister and a secretary for her mission board. She did not realize how seriously young Morris took her words. He had been told that he needed to be educated in America in order to reach his people. Now he was being told he needed to go to America to learn more about the Holy Spirit. The answer seemed simple: Go to America.

Journeying to the coast, Morris found a boat unloading cargo and taking on provisions. He went up to the captain and asked him for passage to New York. The captain cursed at him. "My ship does not carry passengers," he said. "You must be crazy." Morris stayed on the beach for two days while the ship continued unloading its cargo and provisioning itself for the next voyage. Each time he saw the captain, Morris asked for passage and the captain refused. Then one morning, he approached the captain after two crewmen had deserted. Assuming that Morris had sailing experience (he had none), the captain took him on.

Life on the ship was hard. The infuriated captain almost put Morris off when he discovered that the young African had never sailed before, but Morris talked him out of it. Early in the voyage, Morris spent a night in the rigging of the ship during a storm. He swallowed so much sea water that he became ill and collapsed. The captain's reaction was to kick him as he lay on the deck. Morris prayed fervently that he would not get sick again—and he never did—but the voyage was still difficult. The storm had caused so much leaking that the slender Morris spent most of his waking hours for two weeks laboriously working the pumps (and praying all the while) until repairs could be made.

Weather and work were not the only dangers. Once the captain got drunk and struck Morris unconscious. Morris recovered, did his work diligently, prayed for the captain, and witnessed to him. On another occasion most of the crew got drunk. One Malay sailor brandished a cutlass and threatened to cut down the first man he could reach. Morris stepped up to him and said, "Don't kill; don't kill." The Malay threatened, wavered, and then backed down. Morris's bravery impressed the captain, who began to listen to the prayers and the witnessing. He was eventually converted.

Samuel Morris had one sea adventure worthy of *Treasure Island*. Before leaving African waters, the ship approached one area to trade. (An inexperienced seaman, Morris could not tell whether it was an island or a peninsula of the African coast.) Unknown to the captain and crew, a white man had incited the natives of that region. Only a few weeks before, they had seized another ship and killed the entire crew. As the captain set out with a launch loaded with goods, he saw a wave of natives skimming out toward him in their small, swift craft. Quickly, he ordered a return to the ship. The natives overtook and surrounded the launch, but the captain and his men fought them off. Other raiders managed to clamber aboard the main ship, and a bloody battle broke out on the main deck. The white leader of the renegades was one of the first killed, but his followers fought on. The captain, back onboard his ship, locked Morris in the captain's quarters to guard the valuables kept there. In the cabin, Morris could hear the sounds of the fighting and, when the fighting stopped, the splash of bodies into the sea. The ship's crew had repelled the attackers and set sail for the open sea. The captain, victorious but bloodied, finally staggered back to the cabin, where Morris tended his wounds.

A NEW WORLD

Landing in New York, Morris went up to the first person he saw and asked, "Where's Stephen Merritt?" Providentially, the man, a tramp, had been to Merritt's rescue mission. He took Morris to Merritt's office, where the pastor was just leaving for the day. "I am Samuel Morris," he said. "I've just come from Africa to talk with you about the Holy Ghost." Taken aback, Merritt said that he had another appointment, but he invited Morris to stay at the mission until he returned. When Merritt got back later that evening, he found Samuel Morris praying with seventeen men he had witnessed to. Wondering over this unusual young African, Merritt took him home and put him in a guest room. He gave Morris spare pajamas so large that the sight made Merritt laugh—until Morris began to pray. Then the pastor was moved. Stephen Merritt began to realize he had an unusual houseguest.

Morris spent several weeks with Merritt, who took him in, gave him new clothes, and took him to church services, Sunday school assemblies, and revival meetings. In these assemblies Morris shared his testimony, and many Christians offered money to help send him to school. One of Morris's biographers mentions that several times in America whites, at first dismayed at having to fellowship with a black man, rapidly changed their minds when they actually met him and especially when they heard him pray.

Merritt arranged for Morris to go to Taylor University, a Methodist school then located in Fort Wayne, Indiana. The treasurer of Merritt's mission board sent a letter to the school describing Morris as "about twenty years of age." He assured the university that the young man was "thoroughly saved" and had been "doing mission work" during his stay with Merritt. Morris "speaks several African languages and wants to get some education and return to his people," the letter said. "He reads and writes in English, which he speaks quite well." The school agreed, and Morris traveled west to Indiana to enroll at Taylor during the 1891-92 school year.

AT THE UNIVERSITY

The school to which Morris came had begun as Fort Wayne College in 1855 and had only recently changed its name in 1890 to Taylor University in honor of Bishop William Taylor, a leading Methodist missionary. Bishop Taylor had in fact conducted work among Morris's Kru tribe (although he did not know Morris himself), and his board had sent missionaries to that region. The missionaries who had shown Morris the way to Christ served under Bishop Taylor's board. It was only natural for Stephen Merritt, secretary to the mission board, to think of Taylor University as the place to send Morris.

Although Morris did not know it, he came to a school facing serious problems. The new president, Thaddeus C. Reade (1891-1902), was struggling under enormous financial pressure, and it was not easy for him to take on another student unable to pay his way. But Reade was moved by Morris's situation. Furthermore, as Taylor University's official historian notes, Morris embodied the qualities that Reade was seeking to promote in the school. President Reade and the other major leaders at Taylor were supporters of the Holiness movement. Holiness Methodists hoped to call Methodism back to what they saw as the heart of John Wesley's original movement. They desired heartfelt conversion, an upright life, and the empowering of the Holy Spirit for a holy life. The distinctive belief of Holiness Christians was the belief that after conversion the Holy Spirit could cleanse away the sinful nature inherited from Adam. Samuel Morris, a young man who had come to this country to learn more about the Holy Spirit, found a warm reception among these Christians. And his desire to get an education and go back to preach the gospel to his people typified the kind of sacrificial service to Christ that Reade desired his student body to embrace.

Shortly after the African arrived, President Reade made an appeal in a church for support for Morris; he got fifty cents. However, the next day a butcher who had heard of the appeal came by and gave the president five dollars for what he called Reade's "Faith Fund." This gift inspired Reade to establish an official Samuel Morris Faith Fund. Soon other gifts began to come in. Morris himself was a little put off with money raised this way: "No, that money is not mine. That is God's money. I want you to use it for others more worthy than I." Reade nonetheless paid some of Morris's expenses, but the money was far more than was needed for that purpose. With the approval of the donors, the school applied the Faith Fund to the overall work at Taylor. These gifts helped tide over the university through its financial crisis. In later years the fund provided help for needy students preparing for the mission field.

Samuel Morris did not disappoint those who helped him. On his first Sunday in Fort Wayne, Morris attended a local black Methodist church, and the pastor let him have the pulpit. Instead of preaching, Morris prayed. The pastor said afterwards, "I did not listen to hear what he was saying. I was seized with an overpowering desire to pray. What I said and what Sammy said I do not remember, but I know my soul was on fire as never before. The light that had brought Samuel Morris out of bondage in Africa was surely shining into the hearts of our brethren there in Ft. Wayne. No such visitation of the Holy Spirit had ever been witnessed by that congregation."

Morris had a similar impact on the student body. In a student prayer meeting, Morris spoke plainly yet eloquently to the other students: "Bread is one thing, stone is another thing. I once saw a stone with gold in it, and they told me that it was worth more than a barrel of flour; but when I am hungry I cannot eat that stone, I must have bread; so my soul cannot be satisfied with anything but Jesus, the Bread of Life."

With almost no educational background, Morris was obviously not ready for university-level study. He began studying with private tutors and worked laboriously over unfamiliar subjects such as math. He was dedicated to education because he saw it as a means both of learning more of Christ and of serving Him. Whenever he had a visitor, invariably after the greeting Morris would hand him an open Bible and ask him to read from some passage that Morris was studying. As intent as he was on studying, he still looked forward to going home. He told a friend, "When I get back to Africa, I will gather the children about me and they will sit on the sand." Then, Morris said, "I will tell them of Jesus."

Being from tropical Africa, Morris was amazed at seeing his first snowfall. He thought at first it might be the manna that God had showered upon the children of Israel. Taking some of the snow in his hand, he said, "Earth has nothing half so beautiful. God alone has such a pattern." Morris was much affected by the unfamiliar cold weather, though. He became ill in the subzero weather of January 1893 and what began as a cold turned more serious. With the onset of spring, Morris had to be hospitalized, and he realized he was dying. In the hospital he told visiting fellow students, "I was saved for a purpose. Now I have fulfilled that purpose. My work here on earth has been finished." President Reade tried to rally him by asking about going back to Africa. "Others can do it better," he said. "It is not my work, it is Christ's work; He must choose His own workers." On May 12, 1893, Morris's doctor, who lived across the street from the hospital, was mowing his lawn when he heard someone call, "Don't work too hard, Dr. Stemen." He looked up and saw Morris looking out his hospital window. The doctor waved and returned to his work. A few minutes later a nurse rushed out to get him; Morris had collapsed. By the time Stemen got to the hospital room, Samuel Morris was dead.

HERITAGE

The funeral services for Samuel Morris at both the university chapel and a local church were packed. Morris was buried in the black section of a local cemetery in Fort Wayne, experiencing in death some of the racial segregation that American blacks of that period normally faced but that Morris had often been spared in life. Thirty-five years after his death, Morris's body was moved to a more central location at the request of Taylor's senior class of 1928. The class of 1928 also erected a marker:

SAMUEL MORRIS, 1873-1893
Prince Kaboo
Native of West Africa
Famous Christian Mystic
Apostle of Simple Faith
Exponent of the Spirit-filled Life

Morris had a wider influence than his brief life might indicate. His presence at Taylor attracted both funds and students to the school and probably helped save it from collapse. More important, Morris inspired others to respond to the call for missions. Three students from Taylor, stirred by his testimony, volunteered shortly after his death to go to the mission field, and other students followed each year for many years afterward. President Reade wrote a brief biography of Morris that sold over two hundred thousand copies and touched many lives across America.

In short, Samuel Morris became part of a line of Christians whose dedication and tragically early deaths stirred others. In colonial days, David Brainerd, a missionary to the Indians, died young from tuberculosis. Yet his memoirs, edited by Jonathan Edwards, are still in print and continue to challenge Christians for missions today. Félix Neff was a Swiss soldier of the nineteenth century who was converted during the *réveil,* a major revival in French-speaking Europe. His missionary work among the Waldensians of France lasted only four years before his health broke. But the memoirs he prepared while dying inspired others to follow the path of service he blazed. In the twentieth century, missionary Jim Elliot and four others perished in 1956 trying to carry the gospel to the Auca Indians of Ecuador. Yet the story of their work, set down by Elliot's widow in *Through Gates of Splendor,* has moved countless Christians to carry the gospel to the lost.

Native Hawaiian Henry Obookiah underwent an experience perhaps closest to that of Morris. Made an orphan by a tribal war, Obookiah joined a merchant ship as a crewman and arrived in America in 1809. He ended up in New England, where he was converted and then educated. Obookiah hoped to return to the Hawaiian Islands to preach of Christ, but he died of typhus in 1818 just

109

before graduating from a mission school. The published account of his life, however, inspired the first large-scale mission work to Hawaii.

Samuel Morris also represented a small step forward in American race relations, at least as far as Christians were concerned. Because of his remarkable background, he interacted much more with white people than did most American blacks of his day. Without even intending to, Morris demonstrated to white Christians that blacks were not fundamentally different from whites, that their needs and concerns were just as urgent. He broke down white prejudices and misconceptions about blacks where America's segregated blacks would have had difficulty doing so. Yet Morris himself was often blissfully unaware of the fact. He desired simply to know God and to serve Him. And he could not understand why anyone would be concerned about anything else.

For Further Reading

Baldwin, Lindley. *Samuel Morris.* 1942. Reprint. Minneapolis: Bethany House, n.d.

Ringenberg, William C. *Taylor University: The First 150 Years.* Grand Rapids: Eerdmans, 1996.

MATTHEW ANDERSON

1845 TO 1928

The end of the Civil War brought freedom to all African Americans, but it did not bring equality. Even in the North, where slavery had been extinct before the war, black Americans found themselves facing discrimination in housing, employment, and education. Both government and private agencies made efforts to help blacks. The Freedman's Bureau in the South, for example, established schools, set up courts to help defend the rights of blacks, and distributed food and clothing to the needy. Helping lead such efforts, as it had always done, was the black church.

The church has continually played a central role in African American life. Often, the only institutions blacks could establish and operate without white interference were their churches. As a result black churches became the special possession of the black community. The black pastor became a social as well as a religious leader. Many of the best and brightest young blacks, therefore, looked to the ministry as a calling not only for the service of God but also for the support of their brethren in race. There was the danger, of course, that a man might enter the ministry out of a desire for personal prestige. Or another man might care more for the social impact he would have than for declaring the gospel of salvation in Christ. A man who was able to balance the black pastor's role in the community with his duty to God to preach the gospel was Presbyterian pastor Matthew Anderson.

Anderson ministered in the late nineteenth and early twentieth centuries. During his lifetime the black community was divided between the views of Booker T. Washington and the ideas of the "Niagara Movement" (so called because its first meeting was held in Niagara Falls, Canada), led by W. E. B. Du Bois. Washington stressed hard work, self-help, and vocational education to help blacks better themselves economically. Du Bois and the others did not dismiss the importance of these matters but thought that blacks must also pursue higher education and press harder for their full political rights. (The Niagara movement was eventually absorbed by the NAACP, the major black civil rights group that reflected the approach of Du Bois.) Matthew Anderson blended elements from the approaches of both men. He sought to help blacks economically

111

in fields such as industrial education. Yet Anderson himself was a model of intellectual attainment, and he refused to recognize any lower status that others might try to force on the black race.

EARLY YEARS

Matthew Anderson was born in 1845 in Greencastle, Pennsylvania. Thanks to the prosperous sawmills that his grandfather had built and his father managed, he was brought up in relative comfort for a young black man of his day. But he also knew something of the oppression that so many other African Americans faced. The family farm became a stop on the Underground Railroad as his father housed runaway slaves on their way to freedom. From these escaping slaves, young Matthew first learned of the horrors of slavery. "From my earliest childhood," Anderson wrote, "I had been made to feel the wrongs of the slave and the thraldom which rested upon the colored people, free and slave, throughout this country." He learned these things, he said, "from anti-slavery books, papers and speeches which were being daily read in my family, and the prayers which were offered up by my father." He mentioned his father's prayers last, but they were crucial in shaping his views. His devout parents taught him the Bible and showed him how its truths must be expressed in life, not just repeated in Sunday school. Anderson's opposition to discrimination was based not on some vague humanitarianism but on his Christian faith.

It was sometime in his early years that Anderson became convinced that he could best serve God and man through the ministry. "The one thing above all others, which led me to choose the ministry in preference to any other profession was its comprehensiveness," Anderson explained. "There was in it that which would tend to the development of the whole man, soul and body, more than any profession, consequently in my judgment a Christian minister would be in a condition to accomplish more for his fellow men than others." Anderson therefore left home in 1863 to pursue his education. He attended two Ohio schools originally founded by abolitionists—first Iberia College and then Oberlin College. Oberlin had been among the first schools in the nation to admit both white and black students (and was, in fact, the very first college to admit both men and women).

HIS "BEREAN EXPERIENCE"

After his freshman year at Oberlin, Anderson underwent an experience that shaped his life. He thought, somewhat naively, that he

112

could support himself financially by traveling about and giving lectures. Without making prior arrangements, he went to Delaware, Ohio, expecting to lecture through a local church when he got there. The church unsurprisingly had other services scheduled, so he found himself miles from home with little money. He decided to return to Oberlin but had only enough money left to get him as far as Berea, Ohio, on the outskirts of Cleveland. Even had Anderson had the money, the last train to Oberlin was gone, so he went to Cleveland and spent the last of his money for a room in a cheap boarding house.

The next day—having no food and no means of getting home—Anderson went to a black Congregational church whose pastor was a graduate of Oberlin. He was so impressed with the pastor's message that he went up to him afterward, described his situation, and showed him a letter of introduction from the president of Oberlin. The pastor looked in his wallet but offered no money or other help and said, "Young man, a great city like this is no place for you, I would advise you to get out [of] the city and into the country at once." Anderson then went to a white Congregational church and spoke with its pastor, again showing his letter of introduction. This pastor likewise looked through his wallet and, without giving him anything, advised, "Young man the city is no place for one who is without work and food. I would advise you to get to the country, where you will have plenty of work and wholesome food."

By now desperate and growing sick, he walked to the station in Berea and hopped a train like a hobo. The brakeman found him and asked what he was doing sitting outside on the step of a moving train. Anderson said he was sick. The brakeman cursed and said, "Sick, yes I see you are. You are stealing a ride." Anderson poured out his whole story and how he just wanted to get back to Oberlin. With gruff kindness, the brakeman said, "You must come in or be killed," and took him into the train by which he got back to Oberlin. "Here were three men," Anderson reflected later, "two ministers of the Gospel, one of whom was distinguished for his learning and influence, being courted, admired and honored, a Trustee of Oberlin College, the other was a poor, rough, untutored brakesman; which of these think you, exhibited most the spirit of the good Samaritan?"

Anderson called this incident "the turning point" of his life. Previously, he said, he had been "exceedingly timid, and overly sensitive of the opinions of others" and "proud" of his "acquirements and native worth." Now he learned that he must stand up for himself. The incident also revealed to him something "of the coldness and unmercifulness of the human heart even when beating in a Christian breast." Anderson said years later, "We thanked God then, and we have ever been grateful to Him since for convincing us that the human heart is the same whether its earthly tabernacle is white or black or whether it belongs to the aristocratic or despised of mankind."

"This experience broke us all to pieces," Anderson said; "it was literal breaking over the wheel and making us new." He later named his church in Philadelphia the Berean Presbyterian Church. He could have been referring to the Bereans of Scripture, who "were more noble than those in Thessalonica, in that they received the word with all readiness of mind, and searched the scriptures daily, whether those things were so" (Acts 17:11). But he may also have had in mind what he learned about himself, about human nature, and about Christian hypocrisy in Berea, Ohio.

PRINCETON DAYS

After graduating from Oberlin, Anderson went to Princeton Theological Seminary, the most prestigious and most orthodox Presbyterian seminary in the nation. His beginnings there were rocky. He arrived on October 14, 1874, with a letter in hand from one of the professors, Dr. Alexander McGill, inviting him to come. On meeting Anderson, McGill, who did not know his prospective student was black, first thought the young man was looking for work and left him standing as he asked what his business was. On learning who Anderson was, McGill hurriedly invited him to sit down and then treated him courteously. He tried at first to have Anderson room in a local black boarding house, thinking, he said, that Anderson would be more comfortable there than in the dormitories. Anderson replied that he did not come to be entertained but to study and that if Princeton did not want him in the dormitories, other seminaries would have him. The school then gave Anderson a room—what had been a storage room. A white classmate complained, however, and the school gave Anderson a better room. He was apparently the first black student to live in the dormitories in that school.

After that uncertain start, Anderson said that he enjoyed equal treatment the rest of his time at Princeton Seminary. He greatly enjoyed studying under some of the leading orthodox biblical scholars in the nation. However, when he and some other black students took classes at nearby Princeton College, new trouble arose. Their teacher, Dr. James McCosh, president of Princeton College, did not treat them any differently from the other students. But a few southern students boycotted the class and threatened to leave Princeton altogether. McCosh told them to stay or leave as they liked, but he would not ban the black students. The protesting students grudgingly returned to class.

Anderson graduated from Princeton in 1877, then spent two years filling pulpits on an interim basis around New Haven, Connecticut. He took advantage of the closeness of Yale to take classes there, but he was disappointed in the spiritual level of the churches he worked in. He ministered for a time at a prestigious church, but he called it "the old fossilized church, which had the form of godliness, but was dead." He wanted a place to serve where there was spiritual life, where he could do some good and not simply pamper sluggish saints.

BUILDING THE BEREAN CHURCH

The opportunity for Anderson to serve came in Philadelphia. Lombard Street Presbyterian Church, a black congregation in the city, had begun a small work in northwestern Philadelphia, a section with six thousand blacks and only one small Methodist church. Beginning a Sunday school in January 1878, the mission had struggled along. Various men stepped in over the next couple of years to run the mission—the pastor of the Lombard Street Church, a religion professor at a nearby university, and a theological student ministering during his summer vacation. But by October 1879 the mission was on the verge of collapse. When Matthew Anderson came to Philadelphia for what he thought would be a short visit, the supporters of the mission invited him to take it over.

Anderson was uncertain. He had an offer from a church in Cleveland that offered a regular salary; the mission could offer none. Anderson nonetheless accepted the challenge, taking charge of the mission in late 1879 and becoming its first official pastor the following year. At first the mission could barely afford the ten dollars a month in rent for the building, and after three months the congregation could afford to give the pastor only ten dollars a month in salary. (Five dollars of that went to pay his rent.) The church apparently could not always keep up even his small salary and ended up owing him back pay. (Years later he forgave the debt completely.) With such a slow and difficult start, Anderson had doubts. Thinking back to the generous offer from the Cleveland church, he wondered whether he was "not silly for coming to

115

Philadelphia, to take charge of a mission, which could present no better outlook than this?" He answered himself, "Are not the ministers of Jesus Christ the commissioned heralds of glad tidings of great joy to all the world, to the rich and the poor, to the high and the low, to the refined and degraded alike?"

Pastor Anderson believed that his flock must get out of its small rented building if it ever was to prosper. He also wanted to raise their vision above the depressing circumstances in which many of them lived. Therefore, he began raising funds for a splendid new church building. Because his congregation was so poor and because he saw this work as a contribution to the whole city of Philadelphia, Anderson did not hesitate to approach Christian and community leaders who were noted for donating to worthy causes. This fundraising turned out to be its own special trial.

In collecting funds for his church, Anderson had to face the contempt of some wealthy whites who viewed him, as a Philadelphia newspaper put it, "as a poor colored beggar, having nothing himself, representing a people who are very poor and a cause beneath their consideration." On one occasion, when he visited a wealthy lady to ask her help, she did not even see him but simply sent out her butler—with a quarter. Anderson would not take it. Instead he returned to his office and wrote the lady a letter explaining fully what he hoped to accomplish through this work. After receiving his letter, she sent him a much more generous gift. Another time, one "prominent gentleman" (as Anderson described him) listened attentively to Anderson's presentation and gave a generous check. But he made it out to a friend of Anderson's who was white. Anderson looked at the check and said that if the donor could not bring himself to make the check out to the black pastor himself, he had best keep it. Embarrassed, the man apologized and drew a new check made out to Anderson.

Sometimes Anderson faced blatant racism. One well-to-do Presbyterian elder said coldly, "I must tell you frankly that I am losing my interest in your race. Most of the leaders of your people are very assertive, they want to be the social equal of white people. You have come here, and look how you have introduced yourself to me. You said, 'I am Mr. Anderson.' Now what do you mean by that? You mean simply that you are my social equal and I don't care to have anything to do with a colored man that uses such assertiveness."

On another occasion, Anderson was rebuffed by a would-be "philanthropist" who was a high official in the Pennsylvania Railroad. He told the pastor, "Your people have been placed by Providence in a certain niche, and in that niche they have to work out their own salvation, and they should be content." Anderson did not argue with him, but he went home and wrote him a letter. "There is a contentment I grant which is praiseworthy; it is the contentment of which the scriptures speak, the contentment which every man should exercise in the lot or work to which God has called him," he said in the letter. "But the contentment which has been generally urged upon the colored people . . . to be content in a condition which offers nothing higher, is the contentment of the ox or the ass, and is filled with decay and rottenness." He concluded, "In a Republican government like ours, every man should have an equal chance to rise. He should be content with his lot, but his contentment should be that of a student who is only content to remain in a certain position, till he is qualified for a higher." The letter must have had some impact, for the man gave a generous donation to the work.

Anderson's efforts were rewarded when he laid the cornerstone of a new building in September of 1883 and entered the new structure a little over a year later. He delayed dedication of the structure until 1890, when it was free of debt. The Berean Presbyterian Church was a beautiful church building on a prominent street. Yet even that effort was opposed by many. Some said there was little use in trying to build a Presbyterian congregation among blacks. Condescendingly, these critics said that blacks were too "emotional" in their worship to be Presbyterians and would be happier in Methodist or Baptist churches. One white Presbyterian pastor thought it an "outrage" to put up such an elegant structure for a congregation of poor blacks. Anderson felt such attacks keenly, remarking, "It was Judas who bemoaned the waste of spikenard and his spirit is not dead yet."

THE BEREAN WORK

Berean became more than the name of a church. It became an umbrella term for a whole array of outreach ministries directed toward the black community. The church established a private kindergarten, because there was no black kindergarten in Philadelphia at that time. Finding that many African Americans were having trouble securing loans to purchase their own homes, Anderson successfully urged community leaders to establish a bank that would meet their needs. The Berean Building and Loan Association both promoted savings and financed mortgages for blacks.

Knowing the discrimination that blacks faced at vacation spots even in the North, Anderson founded Berean Cottage at Point Pleasant, New Jersey, as a "summer resort." Not only could blacks vacation there at reasonable rates free from discrimination, but they also could attend Bible conferences directed by the Berean church. In 1889 the Berean Institute was born, a vocational school especially aimed at helping blacks moving from the South make the change from agricultural work to the trade-oriented occupations of the North. Berea also ran an employment service for placing blacks in jobs. The church sponsored annual conventions to demonstrate the progress African Americans were making in education and other endeavors. It founded a local chapter of the Women's Christian Temperance Union, an organization dedicated to prohibiting the sale of alcohol.

The breadth of the Berean outreach was a reflection of Anderson's own vision. "Now from the conception of the Gospel ministry, which I hold, I could never believe, that the work of a Gospel minister was simply preaching, in the commonly accepted sense of that term, but that it included everything, which tended to the development of the whole man, intellectual, moral and spiritual." The situation of the black race in America, Anderson argued, required such an approach to the ministry. "A people who have been thus shamefully wronged, and who are yet far from having their just rights accorded, need more than sermons on the Sabbath. They need encouragement in everything that will tend to the development of true man and womanhood; they need help in the practical things of life."

Matthew Anderson, however, did not fall into the error of many preachers in assuming that social relief and educational efforts were the mainstay of the church's work. Anderson indeed called such activity the "preaching of the Gospel most practically," but he by no means ignored the preaching of the pure gospel of salvation from sin. He noted examples of Berea's evangelistic outreach. He recalled, for example, the first convert under his ministry, a widow with two children. Anderson had often visited her, and he came once to find her washing her clothes while tears streamed down her cheeks. "Oh, Mr. Anderson," she said, "I am such a sinner; I feel terrible." He replied gently, "I am glad to hear you say so, my dear sister, for Christ came to save sinners." He shared the Scriptures with her and she was converted. The pastor also scheduled special meetings for the church: "Every year, in the winter and spring, special revival meetings are carried on, which are always attended with some good results, while on several occasions revivals of considerable proportion broke out, and many sinners were soundly converted."

Matthew Anderson once wrote, "It is the Gospel which the Negro needs and must have, if he would have the stamina of life with which to stand." He saw the gospel as a powerful force that not only transformed a man's soul but also uplifted him physically and mentally. Anderson based his whole ministry on that assumption. By the time of his death in 1928, Anderson could look over an array of ministries: schools, employment agencies, reform organizations. At the center of those ministries was Berean Presbyterian Church. And at the heart of the church (and in the heart of its pastor) was the gospel of Christ, which "is the power of God unto salvation unto every one that believeth."

For Further Reading

Anderson, Matthew. *Presbyterianism: Its Relation to the Negro.* Philadelphia: John McGill White & Co., 1897.

Trotman, C. James. "Matthew Anderson: Black Pastor, Churchman, and Social Reformer." *American Presbyterianism* 66 (1988): 11-21.

FRANCIS J. GRIMKÉ

1850 TO 1937

Historian Carter Woodson earned the title "father of black history" for his pioneering work in setting down the history of the African American experience. He originated "Negro History Week," which eventually became "Black History Month," as a means of honoring the black heritage. He wrote and edited numerous volumes dedicated to telling the story of black Americans in all facets of life. In his *History of the Negro Church* he presented the first comprehensive history of the black church in America. Woodson likened the story of the African American church to that of Joseph in the Old Testament. Joseph was sold into slavery by his brothers yet became God's instrument of delivering his family when famine struck. So, Woodson argued, the oppressed black church could provide a rebuke to the materialistic, insensitive church in America. More than that, the black church could become a vehicle for uplifting and reshaping all American society.

Among the many works Woodson published was a four-volume collection of the writings of Francis J. Grimké (1850-1937), a leading black clergyman in turn-of-the-century Washington, D.C. Grimké was an unusual man. He was well educated in an era when many African Americans had difficulty receiving the most basic schooling. His education came, in part, in one of the most doctrinally orthodox theological seminaries in the nation. Grimké believed ardently in the cardinal doctrines of the Faith, yet he was also a fiery and vocal activist in the struggle for black civil rights. His path to prominence was not easy. Indeed, Francis Grimké could relate deeply to the story of Joseph in one way—he was literally sold into slavery by his own brother.

UP FROM SLAVERY

Grimké and his two brothers were born the illegitimate children of a slave, Nancy Weston, and her white master on a plantation near Charleston, South Carolina. There young Frank (as he was known) lived with his older brother, Archibald (Archie), and his younger brother, John. Their father, Henry Grimké, attempted to provide for his sons as best he could under the legal limitations governing slaves before the Civil War. But when their father died

120

in 1852, the Grimké brothers came under the control of their older white half-brother, Montague Grimké. At first, the situation was bearable. With Montague's permission, Nancy and her three sons were able to live in a "semi-free" manner in Charleston, where she took in washing and did other work to make ends meet. She even sent her boys to school.

But when Archie and Frank neared their teens, Montague decided to take them into his household as "house servants"—slaves who were to work at basic tasks around the home. Both boys resented this treatment, believing Montague had broken a promise to his father not to enslave them. They enraged Montague and his wife by pretending to be stupid, incapable of doing the simplest tasks. Montague ordered both of them flogged for their disobedience. Archie finally succeeded in running away and hiding out until Charleston fell to the Union army in 1865. Frank also ran away but was recaptured. The disgusted Montague sold him to an officer in the Confederate army, whom he served until the war was over.

Their situation improved with the end of the Civil War and the abolition of slavery. Archie and Frank returned to their mother and began attending a freedman's school set up by Northerners coming to Charleston to help the newly freed blacks. Frank and Archie impressed the principal so much that she made arrangements to send them North to study. They graduated from Lincoln University, an evangelical Presbyterian school for blacks. Archibald went on to study law and eventually became a lawyer, civil rights advocate, and diplomat, serving as U.S. consul to the Dominican Republic.

INTO THE MINISTRY

Frank, however, decided to enter the Presbyterian ministry. He had given no previous hint of such an interest. His mother had taught all of the boys the Lord's Prayer, and she had sent them to a Presbyterian Sunday school in Charleston. But even as late as his student days at Lincoln, Frank had seemed less interested in religion than Archie. When a revival broke out among the students at Lincoln, Archie embraced it and Frank rejected it. In fact, Archie became so concerned about Frank and so angry at his apparent lukewarmness toward religion that they actually came to blows over the revival.

Francis Grimké apparently left no account of his conversion or his reasons for entering the ministry, but he wrote in his journal in 1918, "I call myself a Christian,—and, if believing that Jesus

Christ is the son of God and the Saviour of the world,—believes that his blood alone cleanses from sin, I am. For I do believe in him, and trusting him for salvation, I am depending upon no merit of my own, but upon his righteousness alone when I shall appear before the bar of God to render up my account."

Francis Grimké chose to attend Princeton Theological Seminary, one of the most prestigious seminaries of his day. He was one of a handful of black students attending the school. Only a year before he came, Matthew Anderson had become Princeton's first black student to live in the school dormitories. Grimké was in the last class of students to sit for three years of systematic theology under Charles Hodge, one of the most famous and most learned orthodox theologians in American history. How Princeton influenced his theology may be judged by a comment he made in 1928, on the fiftieth anniversary of his entering the ministry: "The findings of the higher critics; the rationalistic tendencies within the church . . . ; the dogmatic and arrogant assumptions and declarations of science, that would banish God from the universe or limit his power . . . have not affected in the least my perfect faith in the Bible."

Grimké spent most of his career as pastor of the Fifteenth Street Presbyterian Church in Washington, D.C. (1878-85, 1889-1928). The only interruption was a brief pastorate in Jacksonville, Florida (1885-89), where he went for the sake of his health. In addition to his preaching ministry, Grimké wrote articles and pamphlets on religious and social issues. He also served as a trustee of both Howard University and the public school system of Washington, D.C. His life was one of service to his church, to those of his own race, and to his community.

ORTHODOX AND PROGRESSIVE

Throughout his career, Francis Grimké defied easy categorization. On the one hand, he was rigorously orthodox in theology. In 1936 he wrote in his diary, "I accept, and accept without reservation, the Scriptures of the Old and New Testaments as God's Word, sent to Adam's sinful race and pointing out the only way by which it can be saved. . . . Without the Holy Scriptures and what they reveal, there is no hope for humanity. To build on anything else is to build on the sand." He has also been labeled a "Negro Puritan" for his strict moral views, such as his constant warnings about immodest clothing, use of tobacco, and attending the theater. He wrote in his diary in 1929, "Rum, women, the love of money, and worldly pleasures, are now, and have been the main gateways to hell."

Yet Grimké was unsparingly vocal about social issues. In 1899 he preached an uncompromising series of sermons against lynching and the apparent unwillingness of government authorities to do anything about it. During World War I, Grimké was lukewarm in his support of the war, noting that a black risking his life for his country as a soldier in Europe could not "enter a single restaurant, eating place, or hotel on Pennsylvania Avenue and get a sandwich, or a glass of milk, simply because of the color of his skin." When he saw white authorities reluctant to defend blacks attacked during the Atlanta race riots of 1906, he created a stir by urging blacks to take up arms in self-defense. In a 1905 address Grimké declared, "I belong to what may be called the radical wing of the race, on the race question: I do not believe in compromises, in surrendering, or acquiescing, even temporarily, in the deprivation of a single right, out of deference to an unrighteous public sentiment." Later in the address he said, "Sometimes, we are told, that it would be better to say less about our rights, and more about our duties. No one feels more the importance of emphasizing our duties than I do . . . but among the duties that I have always emphasized, and still emphasize, is the duty of standing up squarely and uncompromisingly for our rights."

Grimké's strong views, both social and religious, showed in his positions on contemporary civil rights issues. Like many well-educated black leaders, Grimké criticized Booker T. Washington, saying that Washington was accommodating racist attitudes by stressing only the economic development of the race and charging that he was more interested in building up his own power base. Grimké warmly supported W. E. B. Du Bois and joined him in launching the National Association for the Advancement of Colored People (NAACP) to fight to secure equal rights for African Americans. Yet he still cautioned, "Men like Du Bois, when they speak on economics, or on the civil and political rights of the Negro as an American citizen, speak with authority and may be safely followed; but when it comes to religion and morality, they are sadly in need of guidance themselves. They are far, far out of the way as tested by the Word of God and the ideals and principles of Jesus Christ. Their views are distorted, perverted, erroneous. To follow them is to be misled, to be facing in the wrong direction."

Sometimes Grimké's social and religious views meshed perfectly. He supported Prohibition as a means of both uplifting blacks and warring against sin. He said, "When I think of the sad inheritance which slavery has entailed upon the race, of the low moral plane upon which it left it, and then think of what the saloon is doing to sink it lower, do you wonder when I tell you, that as a race-loving Negro, I hate it with perfect hatred . . . because it is making criminals and vagabonds of many of my race. I hate it because it is undermining the foundation upon which alone you can make a strong, self-respecting race; because it is a debasing, character-destroying institution."

CONTENDING WITH THE ORTHODOX

While serving in Jacksonville, Florida, Grimké criticized the famous evangelist D. L. Moody for what he saw as inconsistency and hypocrisy. In his heyday, Moody was probably the best-known evangelist in America, holding campaigns in major U. S. cities. He had originally tried to hold racially integrated evangelistic campaigns in the South and had reprimanded whites who, Moody said, "might possibly be astonished some day to see these blacks marching into the kingdom of heaven while they themselves were shut out." But fierce opposition caused Moody to modify his stance and hold segregated campaigns. When Grimké learned that in Jacksonville Moody was holding segregated services (seven for whites and one for blacks), he wrote, "It is impossible to contemplate this man . . . without mingled feelings of pity and disgust." He said that Moody needed to learn that "the soul of the Negro is as precious in God's sight as that of the white man."

Yet, after Moody's death, Grimké praised the evangelist as "one of the greatest soul-winners of the world." Years later he wrote of Moody in his diary, "He was ever looking out for opportunities to point men to Jesus, the Lamb of God, whose blood cleanses from all sin. That was his business; he had no other, lived for no other purpose. And hence the tremendous work which he did, and the wonderful success which attended his efforts." Whatever their differences, Grimké saw that he and Moody shared a common concern for pointing the lost to Christ.

Grimké's relations with another famous evangelist, Billy Sunday, were even stormier. After the death of Moody, Sunday took his place as America's foremost evangelist, carrying on Moody's work of preaching the gospel to the nation's largest cities. When he heard that Sunday was going to hold an evangelistic campaign in Washington, D.C., Grimké wrote the evangelist to urge him to condemn racial prejudice as he denounced the sins of America. "I notice that you have been striking with sledge-hammer blows some of the great evils of today—intemperance, impurity, gambling, the lust for gold, frivolity, political corruption, the tobacco habit, and the like," he wrote to Sunday. "Will it be asking too much of you to turn for a moment to this gigantic evil, RACE PREJUDICE, and deal it also one of those sledge-hammer blows?"

When Sunday's campaign came and went without a mention of the evils of prejudice, Grimké published a pamphlet angrily denouncing the evangelist: "This man, Rev. Billy Sunday, at times, seems to be a little courageous, judged by his vigorous denunciation of many sins; but when it comes to this big devil of race prejudice, the craven in him comes out; he cowers before it; he is afraid to speak out. . . . What are you afraid of Mr. Sunday?"

Despite his deep disappointment with Sunday on this issue, Grimké still quoted the evangelist with approval when he denounced sins such as immodest dress or praised the importance of godly mothers. Once Grimké quoted Sunday describing "the whiskey gang" as "that dirty, rotten, stinking bunch of moral assassins." The pastor added, "That sounds very much like Billy, and it sounds a little harsh, perhaps, but it is true." Despite his disappointment with the evangelist, Grimké could recognize that they still shared much in common—a fact that may have heightened his disappointment at the evangelist's failure to address racial prejudice.

Fighting Segregation in the Church

Francis Grimké did not ignore the church's responsibility to deal with racial prejudice within its own walls. He lived in a time of increasing racial segregation, the era of Jim Crow laws that forced black Americans to ride in separate train cars, drink from separate water fountains, use separate public restrooms. Grimké opposed this trend, and nowhere did he oppose it more vigorously than in the church. "Think of Christian men and women drawing the color line on a brother or sister!" he said. "Think of Christian men and women standing idly by, and often taking part in the murder of a fellow human being by a band of lynchers! Think of Christian men and women sanctioning the Jim Crow car and all the other forms of segregation practiced against colored people!" On one occasion Grimké's disgust with the behavior of many white Christians led him to declare, "If Jesus Christ should come in the guise of a black man, they would not listen to him, they would not permit him to occupy their pulpits."

One incident clearly illustrates Grimké's view on the church and racial prejudice. In 1904 the Presbyterian Church in the U.S.A.

debated a union with the Cumberland Presbyterian Church. As a condition of union, this southern-based group wanted racially segregated presbyteries. Grimké led a valiant but vain fight to halt the merger until the Cumberland Presbyterians had repudiated segregation. As he said on another occasion, "Organic union is a good thing, but it is by no means the most important thing. It is better to do right than to be organically united." After listening to an impassioned plea by Grimké on the issue, Supreme Court justice and Presbyterian layman John Harlan said, "Let us stand in the way of the fathers, and say to the world that as far as our church is concerned, we are race blind and color blind." However, the merger— with its segregated presbyteries—went through anyway.

Likewise, when the American Bible Society proposed a racially segregated pageant to celebrate its one-hundredth anniversary, Grimké wrote, "Think of a Bible Society drawing the color line! I could not help feeling: If this Book has had no more effect upon those among whom it has been circulated by the Society than it has had upon these men, of what value is a Bible society? What is the use of circulating the Word?" Grimké believed that it is the church's "duty to seek to mould public sentiment in accordance with Christian principles, and not to be moulded by it."

"THINK ON THESE THINGS"

Grimké saw no conflict between his political ideology and his faith, but he clearly saw his faith as the controlling and dominating element in his life. "A minister's first duty is to his own church and congregation," he said. "No outside interests or engagements should be allowed to interfere with the full discharge of his duties on the inside. . . . If a minister can attend to his duties as they ought to be attended to, and yet has time for outside matters, well; but not otherwise." The note of Christian faith was never absent from his words. In 1916 he met with P. B. S. Pinchback, a noted statesman in the black community and former lieutenant governor of Louisiana during Reconstruction. Afterwards Grimké wrote to Pinchback to urge on him the claims of the gospel: "We cannot go into eternity with our sins unrepented of and hope for any good. The blood of Jesus Christ alone cleanses from sin." He closed the letter: "Don't allow life to pass without making the great surrender of yourself to Jesus Christ."

It is not certain that Francis Grimké had a "life's verse," as the phrase is commonly understood. But he often quoted a favorite verse, Philippians 4:8—"Finally, brethren, whatsoever things are true, whatsoever things are honest, whatsoever things are just, whatsoever things are pure, whatsoever things are lovely, whatsoever things are of good report; if there be any virtue, and if there be any praise, think on these things." He viewed this verse, as have many Christians through history, as a safeguard against sin: "The only way to keep evil thoughts out of our minds is to be always thinking good thoughts. Then evil thoughts will not be able to get in. This, evidently, was in the mind of the apostle Paul, in his exhortation to the Philippians."

In addition to a defense against sin, Grimké saw the virtues listed in Philippians 4:8 as expressions of the highest godly character, the standard toward which all people, black and white, should press. He saw the value of education, for instance, but he said that "brain power" with "no reverence for God and for things that are just, and pure, and lovely, and of good report" could have only an evil influence. In one of his last sermons (delivered, in fact, by someone else because he was too ill to speak), Grimké offered what he called "this earnest call to the race to keep ever before it as its supreme aim the building up of a noble character, following always and only things which are true, just, pure, lovely and of good report."

Francis Grimké retired from the ministry in 1928 and died in 1937. He once read a copy of an address about John Calvin and then wrote in his diary, "As I laid it aside, more profoundly impressed than ever before with the character and work of John Calvin there went up from my heart the earnest prayer that when my life ends here that I too may be remembered because of some things that I have said or done in bringing men face to face with life and its great and solemn responsibilities for which they must answer at the bar of God. To feel, as John Calvin felt, the sovereignty of God, and to get others to feel the same, . . . is a great achievement and will go on working for good long after we are gone." It likely would have comforted Grimké to know that this was how he was viewed by those who knew him. As a member of Grimké's congregation said of his pastor, "He stands upright and down—straight as a Hebrew prophet pointing out the straight and narrow way of truth and righteousness."

For Further Reading

Bruce, Dickson D. *Archibald Grimké: Portrait of a Black Independent.* Baton Rouge: Louisiana State University Press, 1993. A biography of Francis Grimké's older brother that also is useful for studying Francis Grimké, especially his early years.

Ferry, Henry Justin. "Racism and Reunion: A Black Protest by Francis James Grimké." *Journal of Presbyterian History* 50 (Summer 1972): 77-88.

Grimké, Francis J. *The Works of Francis James Grimké.* Edited by Carter Woodson. Washington: The Associated Publishers, 1942. 4 vols.

Olmstead, Clifton E. "Francis James Grimké (1850-1937): Christian Moralist and Civil Rights." In *Sons of the Prophets: Leaders in Protestantism from Princeton Seminary,* edited by Hugh T. Kerr. Princeton: Princeton University Press, 1963, pp. 161-75.

Sidwell, Mark. "Francis Grimké and the Fundamentalists." *Biblical Viewpoint* vol. 32, no. 1 (April 1998): 79-91.

———. "Francis Grimké and the Value and Limits of Carter Woodson's Model of the Progressive Black Pastor." *Fides et Historia* vol. 32, no. 1 (Winter-Spring 2000): 99-117.

CHARLES TINDLEY

Before the Civil War and for several years afterwards, most American blacks lived in the South, the region where they had lived as slaves, and it was the place they stayed when they were freed. Eventually, though, the United States saw a shift in the black population. Pushing blacks northward were the economic poverty and racial discrimination that so many experienced in the South. Drawing them northward were job opportunities in the expanding, industrial North.

This migration strained the resources of the black community in the North. Finding jobs took time and effort, and the migrating blacks had to find housing while they looked for jobs. The black churches of the North stood ready and eager to help. They offered aid to their brethren facing the difficult transition to life in the big cities of the North. But these churches were not simply social-service centers and fellowship halls. For the saved, they offered Christian fellowship. For the unsaved, who had needs greater than just housing or employment, they offered the gospel of salvation through Christ. Many of these churches were small congregations, not unlike the churches of the rural South. Some of them became large works, able to extend their ministry to an ever-widening circle of people.

Among the most notable of the pastors of these large churches was Charles A. Tindley of Philadelphia. Like many blacks, he had left the South to find a better life in the North. He had found much more there, however, for he found Christ. He knew the needs and hopes of his people and was able to minister sympathetically to them. Tindley did all of this work with a sense of dependence on God. His theme in life is well illustrated by a song he wrote entitled "Stand by Me." As long as God stood beside him, helping him, strengthening him, and giving him wisdom, Charles Tindley knew that he could overcome all obstacles.

EARLY YEARS

When the storms of life are raging,
Stand by me;
When the storms of life are raging,
Stand by me.
When the world is tossing me
Like a ship upon the sea,
Thou who rulest wind and water,
Stand by me.

Charles Albert Tindley was born on July 7, 1851, the child of slaves living in Berlin, Maryland. His mother died when he was but two years old, and Tindley could not remember her. He described the difficulties of his childhood:

> My father was poor as it relates to this world's goods, but was rich in the grace of God. He was unable to send me to school or to keep me with him at his little home. It therefore became my lot to be "hired out," wherever father could place me. The people with whom I lived were not all good. Some of them were very cruel to me. I was not permitted to have a book or go to church. I used to find bits of newspaper on the roadside and put them in my bosom (for I had no pockets), in order to study the A, B, C's from them. During the day I would gather pine knots, and when the people were asleep at night I would light these pine knots, and, lying flat on my stomach to prevent being seen by any one who might still be about, would, with fire-coals, mark all the words I could make out on these bits of newspaper. I continued in this way, and without any teacher, until I could read the Bible almost without stopping to spell the words.

At least some of his masters must have allowed Tindley to attend church. He recalled how one Sunday as a boy, after he had finished his chores in the morning, he decided to go to church. On the way there, he noticed that his bare feet were dirty, so he "washed" them in ditch water and dried them with leaves. He sat in the back of the church, but when the speaker asked for all boys and girls who could read the Bible to come to the front seat, he went forward. He recalled the odd looks the people gave him, and he heard whispers about the "boy with the bare feet." Tindley said, "From that moment my ambition to be educated knew no bounds. I would plow all day in the field and walk and run fourteen miles at night going and coming to get the school teacher who was kind enough to give me lessons."

130

In his sermons years later, Tindley recalled some scenes from his childhood that show a happier side of his early years. He remembered walking through a beautiful field of ripened wheat with his father. He asked whether they could just not reap the wheat so that Charles and his dog, Nero, could keep on playing there. His father looked at him "pityingly" (as Tindley recalled) and replied, "I must cut this wheat in order to give you bread to eat." Once, while preaching on "God's husbandry," he related how his father had given him a little patch in which to grow corn. He related with pride how he had planted and tended the corn until he finally harvested it. In another sermon, while illustrating kindness without wisdom, he noted how his father had once given him an egg to have hatched so that Tindley could have his own chicken. When the chick seemed to be taking too long to hatch under the setting hen, he cracked the shell slightly to "help." Of course, the chick died. These scenes, and others, reveal a childhood that was hard and certainly poor, but one marked by love and warmth.

SALVATION AND THE MINISTRY

In the midst of tribulations,
Stand by me;
In the midst of tribulations,
Stand by me.
When the hosts of hell assail,
And my strength begins to fail,
Thou who never lost a battle,
Stand by me.

The Civil War ended when Tindley was a teenager, and he found freedom with adulthood. He became a manual laborer, and he met and married Daisy Henry. Tindley and his new bride went to Philadelphia to try to make a better living. He worked during the day and went to school at night. He began attending a Methodist church in town, and there he was converted to Christ. Tindley began his service for Christ in a humble way: he became the church janitor. With the encouragement of his pastor, Tindley continued to study. As someone remarked who knew him at this time, "He seems nice, but he don't get his head out of a book long enough to let you know him." As he studied, Tindley began to seriously consider the ministry.

Later in life, Tindley described his education from his days as a church janitor to his early years in the ministry:

My first plan was to buy every book I could which I thought contained anything that I should know. Then I entered by correspondence, all the schools which my limited means would afford, and sought to keep up the studies with any pupil who studied in the school room. I was able to attend the Brandywine Institute and to finish its Theological course. By correspondence, I took the Greek course through the Boston Theological School and the Hebrew . . . through the Hebrew synagogue on North Broad Street. . . . I took my studies in Science and Literature as a private student because I was unable to attend the Universities where these subjects were taught. Thus, while I was unable to go through the schools, I was able to let the schools go through me.

Many African Americans served as pastors in black denominations, such as the African Methodist Episcopal Church. Others, however, labored in predominantly white denominations that nonetheless contained many blacks on their rolls. The latter was the case with Tindley. In 1885 he took the examination to be admitted to the ministry of the Methodist Episcopal Church, North. Other, more educated men taking the exam were a little puzzled by this apparently unlearned candidate. One asked Tindley, "How do you expect to pass your examination? The other candidates and I have diplomas. What do you hold?" Tindley replied, "Nothing but a broom." But he ended up with the second highest score on the test.

For the next fifteen years or so, Tindley served churches in Delaware, New Jersey, and Maryland. He also worked as a home missionary, helping establish new congregations. From 1899 to 1902 he served as presiding elder of the Wilmington District of the Methodist Episcopal Church, North, an important administrative job. Then in 1902, Charles Tindley became pastor of Bainbridge Street Methodist Church in Philadelphia, the very church in which he had been converted and had served as a janitor.

MINISTRY IN PHILADELPHIA

In the midst of faults and failures,
Stand by me;
In the midst of faults and failures,
Stand by me.
When I do the best I can,
And my friends misunderstand,

Thou who knowest all about me,
Stand by me.

The church had 130 members when Tindley came, but it grew rapidly under his ministry. By 1906 the congregation had grown so large that it bought a larger building from a white Presbyterian congregation. Since it was no longer located on Bainbridge Street, the church changed its name to East Calvary Methodist Episcopal Church. Tindley's congregation was large, but it was not rich. It consisted mostly of blue collar workers, caterers, domestic servants, and small businessmen such as barbers. Tindley believed God had an important work to do here, and he turned down a promotion within the Methodist hierarchy to stay with his church.

Pastor Tindley was alert to both the spiritual and physical needs of his church and of his community. He organized a building and loan society for his church members to encourage them to save money and to arrange mortgages so that they could buy houses. When he learned how poor the food was in the free soup kitchens for the needy, Tindley committed his church to providing meals for the hungry. "Not one penny is to be charged them," he said. "Our Master fed the multitudes without cost, and if we are his followers we must do the same. Do you remember how it was when we were back home in Maryland and Delaware? Down home nobody went hungry, and just because we are in this big city is no excuse that it should be otherwise." Later he opened one of the church auditoriums to house the homeless overnight in bad weather.

During World War I, the shortage of workers in northern industries drew many more blacks from the South. The black population of Philadelphia tripled and stretched the resources of the black community thin. Tindley organized efforts to find housing for the transplanted southerners in the homes of his own church members. Then Tindley headed up the establishment of a housing committee to enlist other black churches in the effort. So successful was this work that it received notice in the national press.

Charles Tindley also burned with an evangelistic zeal, and he did not urge his people to do what he would not do himself. Tindley often conducted personal evangelistic work on the streets of Philadelphia. He regularly went down to the sidewalks and street corners that were popular meeting places for the black community. Biographer Ralph Jones writes, "Up and down this area, Tindley walked and talked about God's saving grace. Sometimes individually and sometimes in small clusters, these worldly people were exhorted to attend church and to seek their souls' salvation. Counseling and consoling, Tindley moved among un-churched folk. Many . . . cabbies . . . were often aroused by Tindley for a shared moment of prayer. He got to be known as 'Our preacher' as he moved among these people."

Growth at East Calvary was phenomenal. The main auditorium of the church held only a thousand people when packed to capacity. Tindley had to ask members not to attend both services on Sunday so that others could get in. The church clearly needed a new building. With advice from community leaders and the enthusiastic support of his congregation, Tindley oversaw the construction of an impressive new building. The beautiful, spacious structure seated 3,200—and it was still regularly filled to more than capacity. At the congregation's urging, the church was renamed Tindley Temple Methodist Episcopal Church. Yet even this triumph was tinged with sadness. In the early hours of the Sunday in December 1924 when the new building was to open, Mrs. Daisy Tindley died suddenly. Tindley himself was unable to attend the opening services in his new building.

SERMON AND SONG

Tindley's church was built on preaching. Charles Tindley was a powerful preacher. He had a dominating presence with his height (six feet three inches) and rich voice. Furthermore, he had come through poverty and suffering and could feel for the needs of his hearers. The bite of his sermons derived from his strong Christian orthodoxy too, as he strove to present messages, as he put it, "calculated to confirm and strengthen . . . all who believe in God and in the inerrancy of the Holy Bible." The Bible was the key to meeting needs, Tindley said. In one sermon, the preacher listed units of measure, such as bushels, inches, and yards, and then said, "These . . . are inadequate to measure spiritual things. For this, we have the Holy Bible, the infallible revelation of the unerring and immutable God. Its truths are applicable to all people during all times. . . . No one can go wrong following the truths of the Bible."

In 1915 Tindley first delivered "Heaven's Christmas Tree," which became his most famous sermon. The first time he preached it, over a hundred people were converted, and he preached it many more times in his career, usually in a special December service. The inspiration for the message was an incident that took place when Tindley visited Philadelphia several years before he came there to pastor. He passed a church on Sunday morning where he

134

saw someone on a ladder taking packages off a Christmas tree and giving them to the children below. He watched one poorly dressed boy walk out of the church with nothing but tears in his eyes. Moved, Tindley followed the boy, who "was kicking bits of paper here and there," until he reached home, "a poor, cheerless home." Now finding himself with tears in his eyes, Tindley said that he prayed, "Will there ever be a time when the spirit of the Christ shall so fill and control the lives of people that everybody, young and old, rich and poor, will receive some token of love on Christmas Day?"

With that thought in mind, he preached on Christ as the tree of life. The Savior "was Heaven's Christmas Tree bearing a gift of rare blessing for every human being in all this world." He asked his hearers to imagine the gifts men could find on this tree:

> Here is *Hope for the Hopeless*. This package hangs on a limb that almost touches the ground. It is the lowest limb on the Tree of Life and is the easiest reached package on Heaven's Christmas Tree. . . .
>
> I point to another package on another limb, a little higher up. It is marked *Forgiveness for the Guilty*. It shines with the brightness of the Redeemer's face and is stained with the blood of Calvary. . . .
>
> I see another package a little higher up still. On it is written *Help for the Weak*. Christ Jesus promises help to everyone who wants to live for God. . . . I want you to see the mighty arm that reaches down over this package to every helpless soul who wants to leave the Devil. . . .
>
> I see another package on a higher limb. It is marked *Friendship for the Friendless*. . . .
>
> I see another package, higher still, marked *Peace for the Troubled Soul*. . . . Oh, no, my friends, I am not trying to make you believe that because you have religion you are going to heaven on flowery beds of ease, but I am happy to tell you that there is a promise of sweet peace to all the children of God. . . .
>
> There is just one more package that I wish to mention tonight. It hangs on the top limb of Heaven's Christmas Tree. So bright is the light that shines upon it one cannot see it with physical eyesight. You will have to see it with the eyes of faith, for it is spiritually discerned. . . .
>
> On this top-limbed package are the words *Home for the Homeless*. . . . I want you to fix your eyes toward the top limb of this Heaven's Christmas Tree and [read] the title of the

package which is near enough to the homeland of the soul to catch the light of that eternal sun. . . .

I rejoice with you in the prospect of that great home-coming in the sweet by and by, where no children will mourn the loss of mothers, no funeral dirges are sung, nor farewell tears are shed and nobody will ever say good-bye.

Tindley was known not only as a preacher but also as a hymn writer. It was sometimes ordinary events and encounters that inspired the writing of his songs. According to one account, Tindley composed "Nothing Between" when the wind blew a piece of paper between the lamp and Tindley as he sat writing a sermon. This trivial, commonplace incident set him to thinking about the things that could come between a Christian and Christ. The chorus of this song provided both a prayer and a sermon:

Nothing between my soul and the Saviour,
So that His blessed face may be seen;
Nothing preventing the least of His favor,
Keep the way clear! Let nothing between.

Tindley's constant interaction with other people was another source of inspiration. Several times a woman brought the same matter to Tindley for counseling. He finally said to her, "Why don't you take your burden to the Lord and leave it there?" This event led him to write "Leave It There":

Leave it there, leave it there,
Take your burden to the Lord and leave it there;
If you trust and never doubt,
He will surely bring you out;
Take your burden to the Lord and leave it there.

Sometimes his songs were born of some deep, personal trial. In a sermon, for instance, Tindley said, "It was when I was overburdened with criticisms, abuse and hard and many oppositions—some of them from those whom I took to be my best friends—I wrote 'Stand by Me.'" That song has since comforted many who felt "the storms of life . . . raging" in their own lives.

"Nothing Between" is perhaps Tindley's most famous hymn, although some hymnologists think "We'll Understand It Better By and By" (also known as "By and By" and "When the Morning Comes") might be more widely known. Tindley's work also became the basis for an even more notable song. Around 1900 he wrote "I'll Overcome Some Day":

This world is one great battle-field,
With forces all arrayed;
If in my heart I do not yield
I'll overcome some day. . . .

Both seen and unseen power join
To drive my soul astray,
But with His Word a sword of mine,
I'll overcome some day.

This song, with its theme of triumph over adversity through Christ, became the inspiration for "We Shall Overcome," the anthem of the civil rights movement in the 1950s and 1960s. As extensive as Tindley's ministry was in Philadelphia, it could not match the outreach that his music has had, even to Christians barely aware of his name.

TROUBLES AND TRIALS

In the midst of persecution,
Stand by me;
In the midst of persecution,
Stand by me.
When my foes in battle array,
Undertake to stop my way,
Thou who saved Paul and Silas,
Stand by me.

As a black man, Tindley occasionally faced opposition, even violence, because of his race. Tindley said in one sermon, "Previous conditions of servitude, in the eyes of our enemies, have left its ineffaceable marks of inferiority upon every human being whose veins contain one drop of Negro blood. The proud Anglo-Saxons have been taught that they are the recipients of creative superiority fixed indelibly upon that race by the hand of the eternal Creator." The pastor experienced this contempt firsthand when he led a demonstration at the premiere of the film *Birth of a Nation* (1915). Although this motion picture is considered a classic work, blacks were offended by its glorification of the Ku Klux Klan and its demeaning portrayal of African Americans. The protest was broken up when a mob attacked the group. Tindley suffered only minor injuries but some of the protesters ended up in the emergency room.

Not all the opposition Tindley faced was by any means racially motivated. One of the most discouraging encounters he experienced came at the hands of a fellow black minister. The Methodist Church began discussing the possibility of making Tindley a

137

bishop. A better educated black preacher opposed the idea, thinking that he should get the position. This minister confronted Tindley and said, "You are an unlettered ignoramus. You know you are not educationally fit to be a bishop." Tindley replied, "God does not know that." Just before the vote to elect a bishop was to be conducted, someone distributed an anonymous letter accusing Tindley of immorality. It is impossible to gauge exactly what impact the letter had, but Tindley lost the election.

Often trials arose within his own family circle. He was deeply saddened when one of his sons was killed in action in World War I. Then Tindley's daughter Emmaline became pregnant out of marriage. Tindley stood by her and kept her and her new son Nathaniel in the home. She overcame this hurdle and later married a young Methodist minister. But people within and without the church criticized her—and Tindley too. After his wife died, Tindley found that he had much more trouble with conflicts between his grown children, many of whom still lived in the family home. When Tindley married again, to the widow of another Methodist minister, several of his children took a dislike to their new stepmother and did not hide the fact. The pastor finally sent them out of the house, resulting in greater peace at least at home.

The glorious new building for Tindley Temple Methodist Church took a financial toll. Tindley's flock was large, but it was not wealthy. Mortgage payments and upkeep were a tremendous drain. He told them on one occasion when the financial pressure was great: "All of us know we are without jobs. We don't own big bank accounts. We don't even know what tomorrow will bring. But we do have hope. We do have God. We do have salvation. We do have faith." The people gave sacrificially to help the church, but their small incomes and the coming of the Great Depression made finances a constant worry.

This financial situation caused the trustees and members of the church to call in, over Tindley's objections, evangelist G. Wilson Becton and his "World's Gospel Feast Party." Becton promised dramatic increases in both numbers and giving. Tindley fought the idea, saying, "I won't have this church contaminated by these people. They use worldly gimmicks to entice money from others, which they then squander instead of advancing the cause of Christ." But the church leaders felt desperate, and they also hoped to give the aging Pastor Tindley some relief from the burden of his work.

138

Becton and his staff came in all their finery, offering polished musical and preaching presentations. Becton himself appeared at the opening meeting in morning coat, ascot, spats, and an opera cape. At first, "The World's Gospel Feast Party" was very successful. Large crowds attended the services, and money rolled in (from which Becton got his designated percentage). As the campaign went from weeks to months, however, the offerings dropped. The services attracted crowds of young people, but they came only to Becton's services and gave little money to the church. Finally, the church, to Tindley's relief, ended the campaign. But Becton simply moved to a nearby arena where he started holding services in competition with Tindley's church. Some of the evangelist's dealings, however, aroused someone's anger. After about a month in his new location, Becton was gunned down as he climbed into his limousine behind the arena where the services were being held. The crime was never solved.

FINAL DAYS

When I'm growing old and feeble,
Stand by me;
When I'm growing old and feeble,
Stand by me.
When my life becomes a burden,
And I'm nearing chilly Jordan,
O Thou "Lily of the valley,"
Stand by me.

Tindley obviously took no delight in Becton's death. His own life and work were drawing to a close, and he did not waste his energies on thoughts of revenge. Although he had reached his eighties, Tindley still seemed vigorous to most observers. His final illness and decline came quickly and were not readily apparent. When the pastor came to a hospital one day in 1933, the surprised director of the hospital said, "How are you Reverend? Glad to see you. What can we do for you?" Tindley replied, "I have come to die." In the hospital those last days, he three times said to his wife, "I have told you I was going to heaven." Just before he died, he said, "I am going now."

Charles Albert Tindley died on July 26, 1933. At his death, a journalist reported, "All Philadelphia went into mourning." Through his preaching, Tindley won many unsaved people to Christ and strengthened many believers. Through his outreach to the poor and the hand he extended to blacks coming from the

South, he helped many others who rarely if ever attended a service in his church. Through his songs, Tindley touched the lives of people he never saw. All this Charles Tindley accomplished not by his own strength but by the might of the God who "stood by him" in all the storms of life.

> Thou who rulest wind and water . . .
> Thou who never lost a battle . . .
> Thou who knowest all about me . . .
> Thou who saved Paul and Silas . . .
> O Thou "Lily of the valley,"
> Stand by me.

For Further Reading

Jones, Ralph H. *Charles Albert Tindley: Prince of Preachers.* Nashville: Abingdon, 1982.

Reagon, Bernice Johnson, ed. *We'll Understand It Better By and By: Pioneering African American Gospel Composers.* Washington: Smithsonian Institute Press, 1992. Contains two articles on the career and songs of Tindley (pp. 37-78).

Tindley, Charles. "Heaven's Christmas Tree." *Fundamentalist Journal,* December 1985, pp. 42-44.

CHARLES PRICE JONES

Religious movements frequently arise when a group of Christians feels that some vital truth of Christianity is being ignored by the majority of professing Christians. Often, the result is conflict between the reformers and those who think the reform is unnecessary. In the latter half of the nineteenth century, one such controversial reform movement that arose within American Christianity was the Holiness movement.

The Holiness movement originated within Methodism. "Holiness Christians" thought that the Methodist church was growing cold and formal, losing the warmth and fervor of its founder, John Wesley. They insisted that a truly Christian life must be marked by holiness. Many other Christians who were not Methodists gave a loud amen to this call and joined the movement. Despite some disagreements among different Holiness groups, nearly all agree on the central importance of "eradication," a doctrine that states that the Holy Spirit cleanses the believer by a special work of grace after salvation. Called the "second blessing" (after the first blessing of salvation) or "entire sanctification," this act, they claim, eliminates the sinful nature all people have inherited from Adam. As a result of the Spirit's work, these "entirely sanctified" believers are then able to live in triumph over all known sin.

The Holiness movement affected many denominations, not just Methodism. It also affected different social groups, notably the black community. Many African American Christians, particularly among the Methodists and the Baptists, saw the new movement as a renewal, as a new surge of life within American religion. The Holiness movement left in its wake many new things: new congregations, new denominations, new hymns and gospel songs. Other Christians—and even some non-Christians—opposed the movement. The result was conflict and even violence. One of the major black leaders of the Holiness movement was Charles Price Jones. He endured harsh opposition and faced life-threatening situations for the sake of the cause he believed in. But he also triumphed through faith in the God he served.

141

EARLY YEARS

Charles Price Jones (who normally went by "C. P.") was born near Rome, Georgia, on December 9, 1865, only months after the end of the Civil War. His mother died when he was seventeen, and his father apparently had died even earlier. He later said of his father, "I cannot speak too highly of this man. I love his memory. I had not sense enough when young to appreciate his worth. But the years have taught me his true value." His parents taught him of God the best they knew how, and young Jones developed an admiration for his local Baptist pastor. But he did not find Christ as a young man. After his mother's death, he used his new freedom to wander about until he ended up in Arkansas. There he was converted. With the eagerness of a new convert, he began to tell others of salvation through Christ, and he was formally licensed to preach in 1887. Jones attended Arkansas Baptist College, graduating in 1891, and he taught school and pastored his first church while he was still a student.

Jones married in 1891, and he pastored Baptist churches in Arkansas and then in Alabama. He seemed to be successful, but he felt a lack. "In the year 1894," he recalled, "I was pastor of the Tabernacle Baptist Church, Selma, Alabama, and my ministry with that church and with Alabama Baptist Ministry at large seemed to be accepted and much loved. But as I read my Bible and observed conditions, I felt that we were not, as a brother once said to me, 'toting fair with Jesus.' I began then to seek Him with all my heart for that power that would make my life wholly His, so that I might realize both the blessedness and usefulness of the real Bible religion."

Like many Christians of his day, he had heard of the growing Holiness movement. He paid close attention to its views and finally accepted them. His praying and Bible study climaxed when Jones experienced what he considered the "second work of grace":

> I fasted and prayed three days and nights. He then sanctified me sweetly in His love. . . . New visions of Christ, of God, of truth, were given me. The earnestness of the Spirit was mine. I was sealed in Him unto the day of Redemption. The blessing of God rested upon me—all on the merits of Jesus. . . . For in myself I felt more unworthy and undone than ever. It was the nearness, the eminence, the reality of the presence of God that exalted my spirit and filled me with joy, the joy of the Holy Ghost. Yet it made me feel keenly my unworthiness and the daily need of "amazing grace."

Promoting Holiness

In 1895 Jones became pastor of the Mt. Helm Baptist Church in Jackson, Mississippi. He began to promote his Holiness teachings, with no thought that he was about to stir up a storm. "I had no idea at all of taking up holiness as a fad, or an ism, or a creed, or the slogan of a 'cult,'" he said later. "I just wanted to be personally holy. I just wished to make my own calling and election sure to my own heart by walking with God in the Spirit." In Jackson, he became convinced that he needed to preach this teaching to his people. "This conviction 'ate me up.' . . . Maybe it was because I am like that, an extremist, likely." From its beginning, the Holiness movement had promoted its teachings through conventions and camp meetings. Following this pattern, Jones called the first of several "holiness conventions" in 1896. He invited pastors and laymen who agreed with Holiness teachings to gather for Bible study, exhortation, and prayer. In that year he also published his first booklet, *The Work of the Holy Spirit in the Churches,* a study of the spiritual gifts in I Corinthians 12. Jones's new emphasis seemed to be going forward, but there was opposition.

Many people thought Holiness teaching was heresy and overreacted accordingly. Jones wrote, "I was looked on as a fanatic by some; by others as weak of brain; by yet others as a sharper trying to distinguish myself by being different; by nearly all as a heretic." Jones had tried to make his appeal interdenominational, and, in fact, the motto of one of his holiness conventions was "Denominationalism is slavery." But he was still a Baptist, and some of his brethren did not appreciate the new teaching. Even some members of his church opposed Holiness doctrine. Speaking of a Sunday school convention in 1899 that occurred in the midst of this battle, Jones reported, "There was to be a row raised—something the blessed Baptists of that day seemed to regard as the spice of the program. That was a part of their enjoyment. They took it as a part of their liberty in Christ, but they seldom hurt anyone." In the midst of these ecclesiastical conflicts, Jones endured a great personal tragedy. In 1897 his four-year-old daughter, his only child at that time, was severely burned in a fire and died.

Opposition led Jones to take a serious step. "This persecution compelled us to build another sect, which was not our aim nor desire. We contended that Christ is all." Jones was still the pastor of Mt. Helm Baptist Church in Jackson, and he sought to reorganize that church as a Holiness congregation. A minority of the church opposed the move and with the support of other Baptist churches took the matter to court. On a technicality in the church's title, the state supreme court ruled in favor of the minority. Put out of their church building by this decision, Jones and the majority of the congregation began holding services in an empty store where he addressed the people from the counter. The group went through a series of rented halls as meeting places until it could finally construct its own building.

C. P. Jones at least did not face this battle alone. Along with the majority of his congregation at Mt. Helm Baptist Church, other preachers stood by Jones, joining him in founding churches with a Holiness emphasis. Chief among these preachers was C. H. Mason, who founded the group's first completely independent church in 1899. These congregations formed a new body. At first the group took the name Church of God in Christ. But after about a decade, the denomination split over the issue of Pentecostalism, and Jones and Mason became leaders of rival groups.

After being forced out of Mt. Helm, Jones founded the Christ Temple Church in Jackson, Mississippi, in 1902, which became known as "The Mother Church" of his denomination. By 1903 the congregation had been able to build a church (which housed a print shop) and a parsonage. The congregation enjoyed it only two years. In 1905 a white mob approached the church. Using dogs, they were trailing a black man who they said had assaulted a white woman in another part of town. They claimed they had tracked him to the church. Jones recalled the scene: "The mob got coal oil and set the meeting house on fire; they said the culprit was under it, which, of course, nobody believed at all. It was a piece of malicious vandalism." When fire fighters got to the scene, the mob would not let them put out the blaze. The congregation could only watch helplessly as their new church collapsed in a fiery inferno. Also destroyed in the fire was their print shop, which contained two thousand freshly printed hymnals. Weary but determined, the congregation rebuilt. In 1906 a new brick structure that could seat two thousand people was finished.

EXPANSION AND OPPOSITION

Jones took seriously Christ's call to preach the gospel. To his fellow pastors he bemoaned "the lack of the spirit of evangelism among us." He urged, "May God clothe us with the whole armor and fill our hearts with valor to win souls. It will give us new zeal, a new faith, a new unity of love, a new vision of glory. . . . We have the divine message; let us not fail with it. Let us not take defeat.

Let us not faint. Let us be unwilling to fail with it. Let us not loiter by the way." Jones himself was active in church planting and evangelism. While serving as pastor of Christ Temple Church in Jackson, he also started other congregations in the area, sometimes trying to serve as pastor of several at one time. He soon gave these small flocks to other men to shepherd. Jones also conducted evangelistic campaigns that led to the founding of congregations. A tent revival in 1917 in Los Angeles, for example, led to the organization of the Christ Temple Church in that city.

As the Los Angeles campaign indicates, the denomination was moving beyond the deep South to the upper South, the North, and the West. Congregations were soon flourishing in cities such as Chicago, St. Louis, Cleveland, San Diego, and Indianapolis. This growth reflected the fact that many blacks were moving to find work and a better life in the industrialized Midwest and West. Sometimes the beginnings of these churches were small. Many Holiness (and later Pentecostal) congregations began as "storefront churches," meeting in spots usually occupied by stores in low-rent downtown areas in larger cities. The services of these churches were more informal and the crowds smaller than those in the established black denominations of the North. The storefront churches radiated a feeling of welcome and fellowship to blacks trying to adjust to life in northern cities. It was especially comforting to newcomers that the leaders of these congregations were often transplanted southerners themselves.

Growth was not easy, particularly in the South. Holiness preachers had to struggle against not only the normal opposition of the ungodly to the gospel but also racial strife. This was the era of "Jim Crow laws," when black Americans went to racially segregated schools, sat in racially segregated train cars, and drank water from racially segregated water fountains. There was also the specter of lynching, the slaying of blacks by white mobs who accused them of some crime. One future bishop of Jones's group remembered trying to establish Sunday schools in southeastern Alabama. He was told to be careful when he entered one town because the month before a black man had been lynched and his body tied to an automobile and dragged around the courthouse.

Other preachers faced violence personally. A visiting preacher came to help a local pastor with special meetings in Scott County, Mississippi. The visitor recalled, "During the sermon we noticed that a man would come into the audience and whisper to someone. So the brethren abruptly ushered us two ministers through an open window. Of course we ran. Along the road we saw groups of men some with dogs, some with ropes and guns. Arriving at Brother Nickerson's lodging, we ran through the house and on through the field and were lost in a thicket. So we escaped mob violence." On another occasion, several believers on the way to church saw a group of white men by the road gambling. One said to them, "You shouldn't be gambling, come to prayer meeting." They did come— to drag him out to the woods and whip him.

Yet the violence did not always end tragically. One Holiness preacher was set upon by a group in Lexington, Mississippi. With some fear, he saw them returning later and asked, "Are you coming to beat me again?" But they had come to say they were sorry, to ask his forgiveness, and to listen to his message. Nor should one assume that all white people joined in the hatred and strife. Some offered help to the black preachers, offering the use of buildings or other locations to hold services. Jones reported that after the mob burned his church in Jackson, many white people came forward with gifts to help him rebuild.

Jones experienced these dangers firsthand. In Lexington, Mississippi, someone fired into a revival service Jones was holding, causing several minor injuries. Likewise, in 1900 in McComb, Mississippi, Jones was holding meetings when a white bootlegger fired five shots into the meeting. (Jones noted that the next night the attacker was murdered by one of his companions in the attack on the revival service.) During revival meetings in Jackson, a mob actually approached the house of Jones's host to seize him. But the owner stood up to them and said, "You can't come in unless you walk in over my dead body." The mob backed down. Jones had to fear not only for his safety but also how these struggles might embitter him. He noted in 1906, "I was making a hard fight for righteousness, but needed the renewing of the Holy Ghost to rob my spirit of that hardness that makes a man a 'pulpit scold' rather than a shepherd who gives his life for the sheep in tender love."

PENTECOSTALISM

The Holiness movement had known controversy from its birth. In the early 1900s, it underwent its greatest ordeal, a split within its ranks. Challenging the movement was a phenomenon known as Pentecostalism. This system took its name from the events on the Day of Pentecost described in Acts 2, because Pentecostalism's distinctive teaching was that "speaking in tongues" was the sign of the Holy Spirit's filling. The modern Pentecostal movement had begun in 1900 in a Holiness Bible college in Topeka, Kansas, where students began speaking in tongues. The event that brought the young movement notice, though, was the Azusa Street Revival in Los Angeles from 1906 to 1909. Leading these services was black Holiness preacher William Seymour, who had attended the school in Topeka. Large crowds, black and white, thronged to see displays of tongues speaking and faith healing (alleged healing of the ill by supernatural means). So important was the Azusa Street Revival in promoting Pentecostalism that some historians consider Seymour the real founder of the movement.

Pentecostalism divided the Holiness movement. Some embraced the new teaching, and others rejected it. One who attended the Azusa Street event was Jones's friend C. H. Mason, one of the founders of their movement. Jones and Mason had stood together through many trials, including being voted out of their local Baptist association for their Holiness views. But after Azusa Street, Mason was so taken with Pentecostal teaching that he urged the rest of their young denomination to accept it too.

C. P. Jones opposed his old friend over the new doctrine. Jones personally did not believe that speaking in tongues was an evidence of the filling of the Holy Spirit. He said that such a gift could be "counterfeited" and that the real evidences of the Holy Spirit's filling were faith and love revealed in the life. Therefore he successfully urged the majority of the denomination to reject tongues. Mason and a large minority left. Because the Pentecostal group kept the old name "Church of God in Christ," Jones's group had to come up with a new name. Eventually, they settled on "The Church of Christ (Holiness), U.S.A."

After the split, Mason's group grew dramatically, and by the end of the twentieth century the Church of God in Christ was one of the largest African American denomination in the United States. Despite their differences, Jones maintained a respect for C. H. Mason and even honored him as one of the "heroes" of the Holiness movement. But their disagreements were too great to allow them to continue to work together.

Songs

C. P. Jones made a lasting contribution beyond the confines of the Holiness movement through his music. He liked to sing as a child and demonstrated a natural musical talent. While still a young man, he wrote a song called "Jesus Had Made It All Right," and he sang it in church at the urging of a fellow member. This small event was his introduction to a ministry of music.

During the early days of struggle, Jones said, it seemed as though the Holy Spirit were saying to him, "You shall write hymns for your people." His secretary recalled, "In those days of persecution many of those lovely inspiring, encouraging and heart-strengthening songs were born in the heart of our pastor. Sometimes when they were given him in the night he would have us [the choir] join him through the hours and sing. . . . Often we remained in the church until midnight."

Jones often found reassurance through his music. After the bootlegger had opened fire on his revival meeting in McComb, Mississippi, Jones comforted himself by writing "Happy with Jesus Alone," based on the text "Blessed is the man that trusteth in the Lord, and whose hope the Lord is" (Jer. 17:7). When the mob burned Jones's church in 1905, God led his thoughts back to a song written just two weeks before—

Jesus will shelter His own,
Guide them till life's work is done.
Be not discouraged, the Lord is thy stay,
Jesus will shelter His own.

Other songs arose out of profound internal spiritual struggles. The song "Deeper, Deeper," Jones said, "grew out of my dissatisfaction with my limited ability to do good. . . . I prayed in that song for deeper grace, deeper wisdom, more perfect conformity to and willingness to do God's will."

Deeper, deeper in the love of Jesus
Daily let me go;
Higher, higher, in the school of wisdom,
More of grace to know.

"I Would Not Be Denied" originated during a time of spiritual oppression. Jones vividly recalled the experience: "I prayed in every closet, behind every door; wherever I could hide I went to my knees begging for mercy. But no comfort came. You who have been tried in spirit can understand this. Satan tempted me to despair." Finally, he said, "My mourning became a song. When all the trial was over, thinking of it all one day while alone communing with God and thanking Him for His mercy to me, my soul felt that it must express itself in song; and so was born 'I Would Not Be Denied.' Out of the depths I had come. (Ps. 130) Grace had triumphed. My soul sang unto the Lord a new song."

As Jacob in the days of old,
I wrestled with the Lord,
Till Jesus came and made me whole,
I would not be denied.

The song that Jones considered his theme—and his most popular song in his day—was "Jesus Only":

Jesus only is my motto,
Jesus only is my song,
Jesus only is my heart-tho't,
Jesus only all day long.

Chorus
None but Jesus, Savior, Captain,
None but Jesus help me sing;
Fill me ever with Thy presence,
Jesus, Jesus, Lord and King.

Jones wrote the song in 1899 during the midst of the battles that gave rise to his denomination. It represented, he said, his efforts to claim only the name of Christ. He later used the song for the name of his hymnal *The Jesus Only Standard Hymnal,* which was at one time the official hymnbook of the denomination.

C. P. Jones did all he could to promote music in the church. One of his early hymnbooks contained a section teaching basic music theory "which will be valuable to both country and city choirs, as well as to music teachers," Jones said. "Get it, and learn to sing." In his instructions to music directors, Jones wrote, " 'I will sing with the spirit, and with the understanding also,' said the inspired apostle; which showed that he believed in correct singing, but in the spirit of devotion as well. The heart of the church choir should be prepared for singing as the heart of the minister is prepared for his sermon." For C. P. Jones, music was an expression of the gratitude he felt to the God who had saved him. "Sing unto the Lord, sing praises," Jones wrote. "He is the best friend youth or age ever had. Amen."

LATER YEARS

The years following the split with C. H. Mason were ones of organization for Jones and the Church of Christ (Holiness). As pioneers on the American frontier first cleared the land in backbreaking labor before they could build their homes and cultivate the land, Jones in his pioneering had cleared his land and was now at the cultivating stage. He experienced personal sadness when his wife, Fannie, died in 1916; they had had no more children after the daughter who had died in a fire. But Jones remarried, and by his second wife, Pearl, he had three sons.

In 1927 the church followed the Methodists in adopting an episcopal church government. Now "Bishop" Jones was able to see constant growth, constant expansion of the church he had founded. The church continued its printing ministry. "This is the day of the printer's ink, of the picture, of the radio," Jones said in 1930. "We are too poor to use the radio, but we can use printer's ink." He also found time to bury old grudges. Thinking back to the battles with the Baptist denomination that led to the founding of his church, Jones observed, "This would not occur now for they have advanced in spirituality and tolerance. All discord comes from misunderstanding. We have learned to love one another and some of the most highly and strictly spiritual men I know are Baptist."

Jones became ill and had to have surgery in 1943. He never fully recovered, and he finally retired to California in 1944. During his final years, he was able to visit the church that he had pastored for so long in Jackson, Mississippi. A former member recalled how "with tears streaming down his tired face, he would say in his feeble voice to those of us he pastored, 'Little children, love one another.'" Jones died on January 19, 1949, in Los Angeles, and his funeral was held in Jackson at Christ Temple Church.

"Oh the rest and victory of faith!" wrote Jones. "For the Holy Ghost does not speak of Himself but takes the things of Christ and shows them to us." However one may view Holiness teachings, the goal of Holiness Christians was not to exalt themselves but to glorify Christ and to live a holy life pleasing to Him. C. P. Jones had such a desire and as a result felt great compassion for others. God helped him see beyond the jeers to the real needs of the scorners. "They had a way of mocking me about praising the Lord," Jones recalled. "Men at work would mock me as I went along the street, calling the attention of one another to my nearness by saying, 'Praise the Lord.' This never hurt me or aroused resentment in me, I knew they were spiritually ignorant. So I would say to myself 'Thank God, I've got you praising Him somehow.'"

For Further Reading

Cobbins, Otho, ed. *History of Church of Christ (Holiness) U.S.A., 1895-1965.* New York: Vantage Press, 1966.

Spencer, Jon Michael. "The Hymnody of Charles Price Jones and the Church of Christ (Holiness) USA." *Black Sacred Music: A Journal of Theomusicology* 4 (1990): 14-29.

INDEX

151

Du Bois, W. E. B., 8, 111
Dwight, Timothy, 42, 47

East Calvary Methodist Episcopal
  Church (Philadelphia), 133-34
Edwards, Jonathan, 15, 42, 47,
  109
Eliot, John, 63
Elliot, Jim, 109
eradication, 141

Fallen Timbers campaign, 65
Fard, Wallace. *See* Muhammad,
  Wali Fard
Farrakhan, Louis, 10
"Father Divine," 10
Federalist party, 50
Fifteenth Amendment, 5
Finney, Charles, 42, 84, 96
First African Baptist Church
  (Savannah), 2, 25
Fort Meigs, Treaty of, 69
Fort Wayne, Indiana, 106-7, 109
Fourteenth Amendment, 5
Franklin, Benjamin, 15
Freedman's Bureau, 111

Garrison, William Lloyd, 96
George, David, 25, 36, 102
Gettysburg Theological Seminary,
  92-93 ´
Gnadenhütten, 63
God's Trombones, 9
Grant, Ulysses S., 83
Granville, Massachusetts, 42, 43,
  46, 52
Granville, New York, 52
Great Awakening, 15, 42, 47, 55
Great Depression, 138
Grimké, Archibald, 120-21, 128
Grimké, Francis, 120-28
Grimké, Henry, 120
Grimké, Montague, 121

Hall, Moses, 29
"Happy with Jesus Alone," 148
Hardgrove, Samuel, 81-82

Harlan, John, 126
Harlem Renaissance, the, 8
Haynes, Elizabeth Babbit, 46
Haynes, Lemuel, 42-53
"Heaven's Christmas Tree," 134-36
Hodge, Charles, 122
Holiness movement, 7, 107, 141-
  47
Hosier, Harry, 33
Howsaws, 19
Huntington Connexion. *See*
  Calvinistic Methodists
Hurons, 65

Iberia College, 112
"I'll Overcome Some Day," 136
Indians, American, 17, 18-19, 63-
  70, 109
Iroquois League, 64, 65
Ivory Coast, 102
"I Would Not Be Denied," 148-49

Jackson, Andrew, 49, 50, 59
Jackson, Jesse, 11, 12
Jackson, Joseph H., 12
Jamaica, 24, 26-29
Jamestown, Virginia, 42
Jasper, John, 6, 80-88
Jefferson, Thomas, 50
"Jesus Only," 149
Jesus Only Standard Hymnal, The,
  149
"Jesus Will Shelter His Own," 148
Jim Crow laws, 125, 145
Johnson, James Weldon, 9
Jones, Absalom, 34, 37
Jones, Charles Colcock, 3
Jones, Charles Price, 141-50
Joy Street Baptist Church
  (Boston), 4
Judson, Adoniram, 74

Kaboo. *See* Morris, Samuel
King, Martin Luther, Jr., 11, 12, 13
Kingston, Jamaica, 26
Kru tribe, 102-3, 106

Richmond African Missionary
Society, 73
Richmond, Virginia, 6, 72, 73, 74,
80, 81, 83-85, 99
Roman Catholicism, 66
Rose, David, 42
Rutland, Vermont, 47-50

Sagu-yu-what-hah. *See* Red Jacket
St. George's Methodist Church
(Philadelphia), 34, 36
Sandusky River, 65-66
Second Great Awakening, 62, 73
segregation, 109, 125-26
Selina, Countess of Huntington, 21
Seymour, William, 7-8, 147
Sharpe, Henry, 24-25
Sierra Leone, 23, 25, 75-76
Silver Bluff Baptist Church
(South Carolina), 25
"Sinners in the Hands of an
Angry God," 15
Sixth Mount Zion Baptist Church
(Richmond), 84
slave rebellions, 2, 60, 90, 92
slavery, 3, 4-6, 9, 23, 28, 31-32,
38-41, 44-45, 54, 59-60, 62, 75,
80, 84, 94, 95-98, 100, 111-12,
120-21
Southern Christian Leadership
Conference, 11
spirituals, 3
"Stand by Me," 129, 130-33, 136,
137-40
Stewart, John, 63-71
Sturgis, Stokeley, 31-33
"Sun Do Move, The," 86-87
Sunday, Billy, 124-+25

Tappan, Lewis, 96
Taylor University, 106, 110
Thirteenth Amendment, 5
Tindley, Charles, 6, 129-40
Tindley Temple Methodist Epis-
copal Church (Philadelphia),
134, 138
Truth, Sojourner, 4

Tubman, Harriet, 4
Turner, Nat, 2, 36, 60, 92
Two Logs (Indian chief), 68, 70

Underground Railroad, 112
Universalism, 48-49

Varick, James, 4
Vesey, Denmark, 2, 90, 92, 94
Voting Rights Act of 1965, 11

Waldensians, 109
Walker, William, 66, 67
War of 1812, 50, 65
Washington, Booker T., 111, 123
Washington, George, 45, 50, 58
Wayne, General "Mad"
Anthony, 65
Weld, Theodore, 96
"We'll Understand It Better By
and By," 136
"We Shall Overcome," 137
Wesley, Charles, 31
Wesley, John, 15, 31, 107, 141
Weston, Nancy, 120
"When the Morning Comes." *See*
"We'll Understand It Better By
and By"
Whitefield, George, 1-2, 15, 16,
20, 21-22, 42, 46
Whitherspoon, John, 55
Wilberforce University, 98
Wilberforce, William, 98-99, 100
Williams College, 73
Wilmore, Gayraud, 13
Women's Christian Temperance
Union, 118
Woodson, Carter, 14, 120, 128
World War I, 123, 133, 138
Wyandots, 65-70